# MILITARY LAND ROVER

**1947–2012 (Series I–III, Defender, Wolf, 'lightweight', 101in forward control, Minerva, Tempo, Otokar, etc)**

First published in October 2012

Pat Ware has asserted his moral right to be identified as the author of this work.

A catalogue record for this book is available from the British Library

ISBN 978 0 85733 080 2

Library of Congress control no. 2012940367

Published by Haynes Publishing,
Sparkford, Yeovil, Somerset BA22 7JJ, UK
Tel: 01963 442030 Fax: 01963 440001
Int. tel: +44 1963 442030 Int. fax: +44 1963 440001
E-mail: sales@haynes.co.uk
Website: www.haynes.co.uk

Haynes North America Inc.
861 Lawrence Drive, Newbury Park, California 91320, USA

Printed in the USA by Odcombe Press LP,
1299 Bridgestone Parkway, La Vergne, TN 37086

**COVER CUTAWAY:** *Land Rover Limited*

# MILITARY LAND ROVER

## 1947–2012 (Series I–III, Defender, Wolf, 'lightweight', 101in forward control, Minerva, Tempo, Otokar, etc)

# Enthusiasts' Manual

An insight into the development, adaptation and uses of the world's most popular military utility vehicle

**Pat Ware**

# Contents

**6** Introduction

**10** Origins of the Land Rover

The centre-steer prototype 12
The pre-production Land Rover 14
The production Land Rover 15

**26** Land Rover joins up

Military trials 29
Military modifications 32
Midlife rebuild 38
The future of the military Land Rover 39

**40** Purpose-built military vehicles

Air-portable general purpose (APGP) 42
Series IIA and III 'lightweight' 45
1-tonne forward control 48
Defender 127/130 gun tractor 51
Wolf Defender XD 52

**56** Conversion to role

Ambulance 58
Anti-tank 65
Appliqué armour 70
Command vehicle 73
Fire-fighting 73
Line-layer 77
Special Forces vehicles 78
Weapons mount 83

**86** Specialised vehicles

Armoured vehicles 88
Tracked vehicles 92
Multi-wheeled vehicles 94

**96** Experimental military vehicles

Series I command car 98
Australian OTAL military amphibian 98
'Big lightweight' 99
1½-ton forward control 99
Portuguese Army 1-ton wader 100
Llama 101
Challenger 102
Experimental conversions 102

**108** Licence-built military Land Rovers

Minerva 110
Tempo-Land Rover 111
Santana 113
JRA Perentie 115
Otokar 118

**120** The soldier's view

British Army service 122
Service overseas 129

**130** The civilian's view

Buying a military Land Rover 132
Parts availability 136
Originality 138
Restoration 138
Driving and handling 140
Safety 141
Tax and insurance 141

**142** The mechanic's view

Safety first 144
Tools and fasteners 145
Maintenance and repairs 146
Day-to-day problems and reliability issues 146

**150** Epilogue

**152** Appendices

Identification 152
Technical specifications 156
Documentation 167
Useful contacts 168
Glossary 169

**170** Index

**OPPOSITE Photographed at Defence Vehicle Dynamics 2009, this is the Defender R-WMIK with additional roll-cage armour.**

*(Ian Young)*

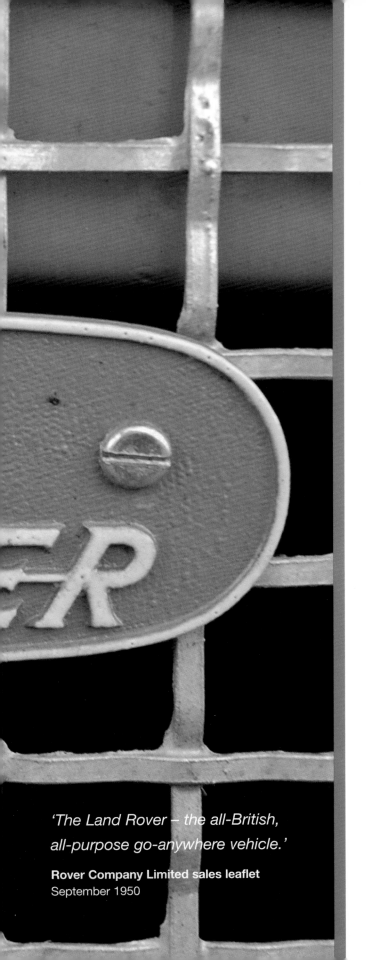

'The Land Rover – the all-British,
all-purpose go-anywhere vehicle.'

**Rover Company Limited sales leaflet**
September 1950

# Introduction

Conceived by Rover director Maurice Wilks, the Land Rover was seen as a general-purpose utility vehicle for agricultural use. Wilks had been using a military-surplus American Jeep around his farm and reasoned that if he found such a vehicle useful, so might others. Although initially seen as a stopgap measure, the Land Rover has remained in continuous production since 1948, with more than four million vehicles sold. And it isn't just for farmers – the Land Rover has become one of the world's most widely used military vehicles.

Not bad for a vehicle that was intended as an interim measure!

OPPOSITE **The familiar 'green oval' badge.**
*(Warehouse Collection)*

RIGHT John Kemp
Starley established the
Rover Cycle Company
in 1878, and designed
the first modern
safety cycle in 1885.
By 1904 the company
was also producing
cars and motorcycles.
*(Warehouse Collection)*

BELOW During World
War Two the Rover
Company produced
thousands of Rolls-
Royce-designed
Meteor V12 tank
engines, going on to
subsequently develop
a smaller V8 version
for heavy trucks in
the post-war years.
*(Warehouse Collection)*

Although no one present can have realised the significance of the decision they were about to take, on 4 September 1947 the directors of the Rover Company ratified the 'development department's proposal... to produce an all-purpose vehicle on the lines of the Willys-Overland Jeep'. Like much of Britain's

motor industry, the cancellation of outstanding government contracts in 1945 meant that Rover was faced with trying to fill a large empty factory that had previously been engaged in war work, against a shortage of raw materials, austerity market conditions across the world, and government controls on domestic sales. As we now know, the Land Rover (as this 'all-purpose vehicle' came to be known) became a huge worldwide success, remaining in production through various changes of ownership, eventually to eclipse and outlast the sales of Rover cars.

## The Rover Company

The Rover Company has its origins in James Starley's Coventry Sewing Machine Company of 1861, but it was James Starley's nephew, John Kemp Starley, who established the Rover Cycle Company in 1878, introducing the first modern safety bicycle in 1885. By 1904 the company had started to produce cars and motorcycles: a separate cycle and motor company was founded in 1906, with the manufacture of bicycles and motorcycles hived off in 1912. The new company's fortunes varied over the years but, by the mid-1920s, things had become sufficiently serious that a shareholders' action committee was established. Colonel Frank Searle was appointed joint managing director with John Kemp Starley. Spencer B. Wilks, who had run the Hillman Company until 1927, became general manager, and in 1931 he was joined by his brother Maurice as engineering manager.

The Wilks brothers concentrated on producing high-quality, middle-market cars, and both production and profits increased during the 1930s. In 1936 the company agreed to participate in the Air Ministry's 'shadow factory' schemes, taking on the running of the first of two such factories to produce components for Bristol aircraft engines. During World War Two, Rover built aircraft and tank engines, and made a huge contribution to the development of Frank Whittle's jet turbine engine. In 1942–43 Rover agreed to pass the work on the jet engines to Rolls-Royce, in return for which Rover would take on the manufacture of the Meteor and, ultimately, the Meteorite tank and heavy truck engines. The Meteor remained in production at Drakelow, and then at Tyseley, until 30 June 1964 when the very last one was built.

In 1944 the Rover management had applied for government permission to resume the development and production of civilian motor cars, but had, at first, been refused. When the decision was later reversed the company decided to move out of the New Meteor Works in Helen Street, Coventry, and to concentrate production at the 'shadow factory' at Lode Lane, Solihull. The first post-war Rover cars, effectively versions of the pre-war P2, came off the production line in December 1945, though the government allocations of steel were scarcely sufficient for proper mass production. New models were planned, including a new 6HP car, known as the M-Type, the smallest car that Rover had ever produced, together with the new P3 which would replace the earlier P2 and would itself eventually be replaced by the P4.

However, difficulties with the M-Type saw that project abandoned, meaning that Rover could not utilise the Solihull factory effectively. The company was faced with trying to survive on the production of just 3,000 or 4,000 medium-sized quality cars a year. Something was needed to fill the gap left by the M-Type – and that 'something' took the form of the Land Rover.

# ROVER

## PROGRAMME

The new Rover cars are now in production. It has been decided to concentrate first on Saloon models. These will be similar in general design to those which were current at the outbreak of war, but a number of detail refinements are being embodied which will enhance the quality of specification and performance long associated with the Company's products.

| Model | Retail Price £ | Purchase Tax £ | Total Retail Price including Purchase Tax £ |
|---|---|---|---|
| 10 h.p. Saloon | 460 | 128 10 7 | 588 10 7 |
| 12 h.p. Saloon | 505 | 141 0 7 | 646 0 7 |
| 12 h.p. Sports Saloon | 520 | 145 3 11 | 665 3 11 |
| 14 h.p. Saloon | 550 | 153 10 7 | 703 10 7 |
| 14 h.p. Sports Saloon | 565 | 157 13 11 | 722 13 11 |
| 16 h.p. Saloon | 580 | 161 17 3 | 741 17 3 |
| 16 h.p. Sports Saloon | 595 | 166 0 7 | 761 0 7 |

Subject to production of Ministry of War Transport buying permit

*One of Britain's Fine Cars*

The Rover Company Limited, Solihull, Birmingham, and Devonshire House, London

**ABOVE In 1946 Rover reintroduced the pre-war P2 with a choice of four- and six-cylinder engines: prices ranged from £588.53 to £761.03, including purchase tax.** *(Warehouse Collection)*

**LEFT Prototype of the M-Type – Rover's post-war small car project. The cancellation of the M-Type saw the Solihull factory lie idle, and paved the way for the introduction of the Land Rover.** *(Warehouse Collection)*

## Chapter One

# Origins of the Land Rover

It is impossible to tell the story of the Land Rover without reference to the American Jeep. As iconoclastic as it was utilitarian, the US Army's Jeep was designed by a team at American Bantam as a pure military reconnaissance vehicle. The first prototypes appeared in 1940 and the vehicle was an immediate success. Series production started in 1941, by which time Bantam was out of the picture. Between 1941 and 1945 Willys-Overland and Ford built a total of 639,245 standardised Jeeps – and one of these utilitarian machines found its way to Maurice Wilks' farm in North Wales.

OPPOSITE **One of 1,500 short-wheelbase (86in) Series Is supplied to the British Army under contract 6/Veh/18599 in 1955.** *(IWM, GOV10680)*

'*The Land Rover is a light four-wheel drive vehicle designed to transport goods and/or personnel by road and across country and for general use in farming operations.*' **Report RT 1/49034, National Institute of Agricultural Engineering** August 1949

The American Jeep saw service in every theatre of operations during World War Two and, like all of the Allies, the British Army received the vehicle in large numbers, although never in the quantities that the Army would have liked. The Jeep proved itself to be versatile and reliable and soon replaced the motorcycle and sidecar, and the small car-based utility vehicles that the British Army called 'tillies'. When military production ended in 1945, Willys saw the future of the Jeep as a dual-purpose agricultural-cum-utility vehicle, aiming the dual-purpose CJ-2A 'Universal Jeep' squarely at the American farmer. Available with a variety of optional equipment, the CJ-2A could be used for tasks such as ploughing, sawing, spraying, welding etc, as well as being driven to town or market.

At the same time, surplus military Jeeps had started to be offered to civilians, and despite often having seen heroic service many were eagerly snapped up by a market starved of new cars. There was even a thriving trade in fitting new bodies to tired Jeeps to produce station wagons, dual-purpose vehicles, small vans and even 'sports cars'.

Like many, Rover's Maurice Wilks was an enthusiastic user of a military-surplus Jeep, having utilised a battered Willys MB around his farm in North Wales with some success since the end of the war. When asked by his brother Spencer how he would replace the Jeep when it eventually wore out, Maurice replied that he

would buy another. This must have provided some pause for thought before the brothers realised that perhaps other people were in the same position. Doubtless aware of what Willys was marketing in the USA, the brothers saw that there was a possible business opportunity and resolved that Rover might be in a position to design and manufacture a British Jeep-type vehicle as a stopgap measure until work could be completed on the planned post-war motor car range.

The decision was taken to press ahead with the construction of a prototype.

## The centre-steer prototype

Work on what was described at first as the hyphen-less 'Landrover' project began at Rover's Solihull factory in mid-1947 under a team led by Tom Barton. Robert Boyle was chief engineer, with Arthur Goddard as his assistant, the latter setting out the production line. Gordon Bashford was responsible for the chassis, and John Cullen was given the role of testing.

There was little time to lose, and development time was reduced to a minimum by basing the prototype on the general layout and dimensions of the Jeep. From a vehicle dump in the Cotswolds, Gordon Bashford purchased two military-surplus Jeeps, which provided a useful source of parts, including a ready-made chassis. Construction of the prototype started after the board meeting in early September 1947. It was completed in little more than three weeks and, although it has not survived, the prototype has passed into Land Rover legend for its use of a centre-steering position – a feature which was certainly not borrowed from the Jeep, but which was selected to avoid the need to develop right- and left-hand-drive versions.

The chassis, along with most of the running gear, was pure Jeep – resulting in the 80in wheelbase of the early Land Rovers, since this was the wheelbase dimension of the Jeep. Surviving photographs suggest that both the front and rear axles were standard Jeep items, and the leaf-spring suspension retained the forged, 'C'-shaped swinging shackles of the Jeep. Under the bonnet, at least temporarily,

**BELOW** At the end of World War Two the British Army retained large numbers of Willys Jeeps. Whilst many were reserved for front-line roles, others were assigned to administrative duties, such as this Military Police vehicle. From 1948 the Land Rover started to fulfil a similar range of roles. *(Warehouse Collection)*

**LEFT** The centre-steer prototype was constructed to demonstrate the Land Rover concept to the Rover board of directors. Although it was powered by a Rover engine, many surplus Jeep parts were incorporated in an effort to reduce the development time. *(British Leyland)*

was the 1,389cc inlet-over-exhaust (IOE) engine of the Rover 10, although even before production had started this was replaced by the new 1,595cc IOE engine destined for the Rover P3. The gearbox also came from the Rover 10, with its distinctive freewheel feature, but was mated to the Jeep's two-speed Spicer Model 18 transfer case. The central steering wheel was connected, via a sprocket and chain assembly, to the Ross T12 cam-and-lever steering box of the Jeep, still in its original position on the inside face of the left-hand chassis member.

In order to keep tooling costs to an absolute minimum the body was constructed, by hand, from aluminium alloy – bringing the dual advantages of reducing the need for expensive press tools and, at the same time, circumventing the nationwide shortage of steel. Windscreen components, brackets and grab handles were borrowed from the Jeep and, not surprisingly, the body had more than a passing resemblance to the donor vehicle, the most notable difference being the use of a bottom-hinged tailgate. On the dashboard, the speedometer, ammeter and fuel and temperature gauges may well have been of American origin, although the switchgear was clearly British. The wheels were the standard two-piece 'combat' type of the Jeep that had been used since February 1942, shod with either the standard 6.00-16 six-ply

Goodyear 'bar grip' mud and snow tyres, or Dunlop Trek-Grip tyres, according to which photograph is consulted.

The prototype was shown to the Rover board on 16 October 1947 and it was agreed that 50 pre-production machines would be constructed prior to the official launch, scheduled for April 1948 in Amsterdam. It was hoped that by securing export orders for the new machine Rover would qualify for larger allocations of sheet steel.

**BELOW** Although the centre-steer prototype was almost certainly broken-up once it had served its purpose, this replica was constructed in 2005 by enthusiast Bill Hayfield, using Land Rover and Jeep parts. *(Warehouse Collection)*

# The pre-production Land Rover

The prototype had proved the feasibility of the concept, but of course it would have been impossible to continue using military-surplus Jeep parts, and the pre-production vehicles differed in many respects from the machine that had been approved by the board.

Most notable amongst the changes was the abandonment of the centre-steer position in favour of conventional left- and right-hand-drive configurations, with examples of both included in the batch of pre-production vehicles. The 80in wheelbase remained, but the Jeep chassis was replaced by a galvanised ladder frame constructed from welded box sections, designed by Rover's Olaf Poppe. All of the pre-production vehicles were fitted with the 1,595cc engine, now with a power output of 50bhp, and there was permanent four-wheel drive to Rover axles via a combination of a four-speed gearbox

and two-speed transfer case with a freewheel to obviate drive-line stresses when driving on hard surfaces. Aluminium alloy continued to be the material of choice for the bodywork, but it was redesigned, with changes made to most of the panels. For example, the Jeep-like side cutaways were abandoned in favour of simple straight-topped doors on exposed hinges, and the one-piece flat windscreen was replaced by the familiar metal-framed two-light design that persisted until 1983, when it was replaced by a single piece of glass in a rubber gasket.

The first 25 of the pre-production vehicles had been produced by late 1947, some of which were rear-wheel drive only. The remainder followed in early 1948, with a total of just 48 constructed in the end rather than the planned 50. The Land Rover was first shown to the public in April 1948, with the official launch at the Amsterdam Motor Show. Road tests began to appear in the British motoring press later that month.

**BELOW In June 1948 the Ministry of Supply (MoS) purchased two of the 48 pre-production prototypes and submitted them to the Fighting Vehicle Development Establishment for trials. The photograph shows chassis number L29, a left-hand drive vehicle.** *(IWM, KID4635)*

# The production Land Rover

In papers submitted to the board for project approval, it had been envisaged that sales might perhaps reach 50, or maybe even 100 vehicles a week. However, with a launch price of just £450, the vehicle was an immediate success, with significant demand coming from overseas right from the outset. In July 1948, some three months after the Amsterdam launch, the Series I Land Rover (as it has subsequently become known) went into production on a line established in previously unused space at Solihull, with additional machining work carried out at Tyseley.

During the financial year 1948–49 more than 8,000 examples were constructed, with the total climbing to more than 16,000 a year later. By 1951 the sales of Land Rovers had doubled, and were exceeding Rover car production by a ratio of two to one.

## Series I

Although the chassis was no longer galvanised, in most respects the Series I production model was similar to the pre-production vehicles. Changes included strengthened doors, improved hinges and handles and modified seats. Conventional one-piece well-base wheels were fitted in place of the split-rim military type. It had originally been planned that the vehicle would be sold in a very basic 'no frills' form, without any weather enclosure, but pressure from customers saw this policy revised and a short canvas hood and side-screens were supplied as standard to cover the cab area. The first batch of production vehicles was sold at the original £450 price, which had been calculated on the basis of lacking such luxuries as doors or a tilt. Subsequently buyers had the choice of a full tilt cover which also covered the cargo area, a full-length metal hardtop, or a metal cab.

A seven-seater station wagon or estate car variant, with a body designed and constructed by Newport Pagnell coach-building company Tickford Limited, was launched at the British Commercial Motor Show in October 1948. Priced at a massive £959, it survived only until 1951, when it became obvious that the government's insistence that it be subject to purchase tax made it too expensive; just 641 were built, with at least one – constructed on a left-hand-drive pre-production chassis – trialled for possible military use by the Fighting Vehicle Development Establishment (FVDE).

It wasn't long before changes started to be made to the production vehicles. In mid-1948 the rear axle, which had come from the Rover 12 car, was replaced by a higher-ratio unit from

**BELOW Although differing little from their civilian equivalent, the first production Series Is entered British military service in 1948. By the time the Series II was introduced in 1958 around 14,000 Series Is had been purchased for the Army and the RAF out of a total production of almost 173,000 vehicles.**

*(Simon Thomson)*

**RIGHT The body of this seven-seater station wagon variant was designed and constructed by Tickford Limited, and the vehicle was launched at the British Commercial Motor Show in October 1948. The first of 641 built was constructed on a left-hand-drive pre-production chassis, and was trialled for possible military use. Sales were always slow due to the government's insistence that the vehicle be subject to purchase tax.**

*(IWM, MVE16782-2)*

**RIGHT** Although details varied from one contract to another, the differences between military and civilian Series Is were often slight and it is said that so many military vehicles were passing down the Solihull production line that the civilian vehicles were painted in the same Deep Bronze Green simply to make life easier.
*(Phil Royal)*

the P3. The gearbox was changed for a similar reason in 1950, and the permanent four-wheel drive and freewheel facility was dropped in October of that year. The Girling Hydrastatic self-adjusting brakes were discontinued in favour of a more conventional design, and the brake fluid reservoir was moved from the scuttle to the seat box. The shock absorbers were

changed so that the front and rear units were of the same pattern. In 1950 the headlamps, which had already been enlarged, came out from behind the wire-mesh grille, and in 1951 the side lamps were moved from their bulkhead position to the front mudguards, and the wire-mesh grille was modified to the distinctive inverted 'T' shape.

Power output was increased in August 1952 when the 1,595cc engine was replaced by a 1,997cc version offering an additional 2bhp and a useful 25 per cent increase in low-speed torque. This engine was not used in other Rover vehicles, but was unique to the Land Rover. In 1953 the engine was replaced by a re-engineered version based on that used in the P4 Rover 60, the larger engine having equally spaced rather than siamesed bores, giving better cooling.

In 1954 the original 80in wheelbase was increased to 86in (2,184mm) and, once again, a seven-seater station wagon was made available. At the same time a long-wheelbase 107in version was launched in both truck and station-wagon forms. By 1957 the 86in wheelbase had been increased to 88in and the 107in dimension upped to 109in; curiously, the long-wheelbase station wagon maintained the 107in dimension until autumn 1958. The extra length was inserted between the toe board and

**LEFT** Wonderfully original Series I with the early lighting arrangements: headlights behind the grille mesh and sidelights on the bulkhead.
*(Warehouse Collection)*

**RIGHT** The Series I also found favour with other government departments – this hardtop vehicle originally belonged to the Home Office, and was intended for a reconnaissance role with the Northamptonshire Civil Defence Corps. *(Warehouse Collection)*

the front axle and made no difference to the cab or load area. However, it was to be a further eight months before it became clear that the increase was required to accommodate the all-new 2,052cc direct-injection diesel engine, and the new 1,997cc overhead valve petrol engine that followed when the Series II was introduced.

The Series I was superseded by the Series II in April 1958, after 172,813 examples had been constructed.

## Series II and IIA

Although visually similar to what was now described as the Series I, Rover's in-house design team had, under the direction of David Bache, made many changes and improvements to the new model. The most obvious was the 1.5in (38mm) increase in the overall body width, manifest in a small curve at the waistline – a

**RIGHT** Lacking its sills, canvas top and supporting framework, this early long-wheelbase Series IIA is marked as belonging to the police service of South Africa. The headlamps moved to the front panels of the mudguards in about 1968. *(Simon Thomson)*

**LEFT** Photographed in West Berlin during the annual Allied Forces Day parade in June 1989, a combined French, American and British motorised colour guard drives along 17th of June Street. A bulled-up long-wheelbase Series II runs alongside a US Army M998 'Humvee' and a French Peugeot P4. *(US DoD, Kai-Uwe Heinrich)*

ABOVE Brand-new late model Series IIA long-wheelbase communications (FFR) vehicle dating from 1970. Note the antenna mount on the body side and the Dexion racking inside the cargo area. *(RAWHS)*

BELOW Privately-owned short-wheelbase Series II. Note the military-pattern headlights, combined with civilian sidelights and indicators. *(Simon Thomson)*

styling feature that has survived in the Defender to 2012. For the first time there were sills fitted between the wheel arches, and a distinctive new engine cover with a curved leading edge appeared in autumn 1958, albeit initially only used on the 88in station wagon and the 109in long-wheelbase variant.

Under the bonnet the Series II incorporated a new overhead valve engine producing 77bhp from a capacity of 2,286cc – although, initially, only the 109in models were fitted with the new power unit as stocks of the old engine were used up.

A new alloy truck cab was made available and there was a whole new range of colours, but the two-piece canvas top was withdrawn. The greater overall width allowed an increase in the track, which improved stability and reduced the turning circle, whilst new, softer springs and redesigned dampers provided some improvements to the ride; the rear springs were also relocated to increase the suspension travel.

The Series II was replaced by the improved Series IIA in September 1961, the design remaining in production until September 1971. The most significant improvement was the replacement of the 2,052cc diesel engine with a more powerful 2,286cc unit, but in early 1962 the long-wheelbase station wagon was offered in both ten- and twelve-seat versions, the latter not attracting UK purchase tax. A six-cylinder

BELOW Late model Series IIA equipped for recovering the Phoenix unmanned aerial vehicle (UAV). The 'drone' is carried in cradles in the rear of the vehicle. Phoenix was withdrawn in 2006. *(Robert Burbank)*

engine option was introduced in April 1967, continuing in production until it was replaced by the 3.5-litre V8 in the Series III in 1980. Another obvious change made to the Series IIA, in about 1968, was the repositioning of the headlamps in the front panels of the mudguards, initially to meet changing legislation in the Netherlands, Belgium and Luxembourg.

The Series IIA was replaced by the Series III in 1971, after 577,967 examples had been built: 126,343 were of the original Series II; the remaining 451,624 were of the improved Series IIA.

## Series IIA and IIB forward-control

The Series IIA forward-control was launched at the Commercial Motor Show in September 1962 on a 109in wheelbase, fitted with the 2,286cc four-cylinder petrol engine. It was rated for a 1½-ton payload, and was said to share 75 per cent of its chassis components with the standard long-wheelbase Series IIA.

In September 1966 the Series IIA was

**ABOVE** Civilian forward-control Land Rover rated at 1 ton. The headlight position identifies this as the later Series IIB 110in wheelbase variant.
*(Warehouse Collection)*

**BELOW** Very small numbers of civilian forward-control vehicles were taken into military service, but this late model Series IIB forward-control was used by the RAF as a radar operations vehicle.
*(Simon Thomson)*

replaced by the Series IIB in response to criticisms about a lack of power. A choice of three engines was made available: the original 2,286cc four-cylinder petrol engine continued in export markets, but it was joined by a six-cylinder 2,625cc petrol engine, and a somewhat underpowered 2,286cc direct-injection diesel. The length of the six-cylinder engine necessitated an increase in the wheelbase to 110in; changes were also made to the suspension, and the axles were redesigned to increase the track and reduce the incidence of halfshaft breakage. The 110in Series IIB can be identified by its lower headlight position.

Production ended in 1973, with fewer than 2,500 vehicles constructed.

## Series III

Launched in September 1971, and easily

identified by its plastic radiator grille, the Series III was more than just an updated version of the Series IIA. There was a new all-synchromesh gearbox, combined with a reduced low-ratio gear in the transfer box – although, in fact, this gearbox had already been trialled, unannounced, in the Series IIA. The dynamo was replaced by an alternator, and the battery was repositioned, under the bonnet. Other changes included a new diaphragm clutch, improved brakes with optional servo assistance, strengthened stub axles and a heavy-duty Salisbury rear axle with improved halfshafts – the last, initially reserved for the six-cylinder models, became standard fitment on all long-wheelbase chassis in 1972. There were also changes inside the cab: the dashboard was completely redesigned, putting the instruments in front of the driver, there was a new steering wheel in a lockable column, and improvements were made to the heating system. Overdrive was offered from August 1974, giving an improvement in fuel consumption.

In April 1982 the 109in Series III chassis was offered with a new high-capacity pickup body, to suit either a 1-tonne or 1.3-tonne payload, the latter fitted with uprated suspension and shock absorbers. The vehicle could be

**LEFT** Standard Series III long-wheelbase general-service cargo vehicle that has been fitted with a roof-mounted work platform, possibly as a helicopter-servicing vehicle. *(Phil Royal)*

**LEFT** Shabby but complete, a camouflaged Series III communications (FFR) vehicle awaiting sale to a civilian owner. *(Ian Young)*

**BELOW** Largely civilian-style Series III hardtop vehicle assigned to the Army Catering Corps Mobile Display Team. *(Warehouse Collection)*

supplied either with a closed truck cab or with a full-length canvas hood, and engine options included both four- and eight-cylinder units.

Production of the Series III continued until 1985, by which time total production amounted to something like 440,000 examples. It was replaced by the coil-sprung Land Rover 90 and 110, later to become known as the Defender.

## Series III Stage One

In August 1978 Rover, now part of British Leyland's Specialist Cars Division, announced that £280 million had been allocated for development of the Land Rover range. £30 million had already been approved for a more-powerful version of the long-wheelbase Series III, to be known as Stage One. Initially intended for export only, Stage One was announced in February 1979, making its debut at the Geneva Motor Show in March, and was available as a station wagon, hardtop or pickup truck, and from 1982 was fitted with the high-capacity pickup body. It was easily identified by its black-painted grille and flush full-width front, and was powered by a 95bhp version of the Buick-derived 3,528cc V8 petrol engine that had been used in Rover cars since 1967, coupled to

**RIGHT** Short-wheelbase Series III showing the distinctive military 'pusher' bumpers, front-mounted towing hitch, and protective enclosures on the front mudguards for the antenna tuning units. The ammo box on the bumper is not a standard military accessory. *(Phil Royal)*

the permanent four-wheel-drive system of the
Range Rover.

A special military version was marketed
under the name Military V8, and examples were
purchased by the Indonesian Army for use by
Special Forces, and by the New Zealand Army
for use as communications vehicles. There
were also a handful of short-wheelbase Stage
One prototypes, but there was to be no series
production, and, as with the Series III, production
of the Stage One was discontinued in 1985.

## Defender

At the Geneva Motor Show in March 1983 the
era of the leaf-sprung Land Rover finally came
to an end when the brand-new coil-sprung
One Ten – or '110', as the grille badge read
– was launched, the second tangible result
of the £200 million investment programme
that had first been manifest in the Stage One.
Despite going on sale in 1983, the 110 did
not fully replace the 109in Series III until 1985.
Compared to what had gone before, the 110
was upgraded in almost every significant
respect, taking advantage of the technology and
developments that had made the Range Rover
so successful. Under the bonnet was a choice
of upgraded 2,286cc four-cylinder petrol and

diesel engines, as well as the 3,528cc V8. The
four-cylinder models were available with either a
four- or five-speed gearbox in combination with
a new two-speed transfer box, with optional
selectable or permanent four-wheel drive. The
V8 used the entire transmission system of the
Range Rover, with an integral gearbox and
transfer case, and permanent four-wheel drive.

The chassis was new, allowing the use of
long-travel, dual-rate coil springs, with radius
arms to locate the live axles; there was a
Panhard rod at the front, and tubular trailing
links at the rear, in combination with a centrally-
mounted A frame. At extra cost the rear axle
could be fitted with a self-levelling system using
a centrally-placed Boge Nivomat strut above
the axle. Front brakes were servo-assisted
discs, and the optional power-assisted steering
reduced the turning circle.

Although there was no significant body
restyling there was a new, and significantly
larger, rubber-glazed windscreen, consisting
of a single piece of glass. Like the Stage One,
the black-painted radiator grille was flush with
the fronts of the mudguards and included the
headlamp panels; there were also body-colour
deformable plastic wheel-arch extensions and,
for the first time, the body cappings were also
body-coloured.

Body options included a pickup truck with
a full-length canvas top or steel cab, high-
capacity pickup with a wider and longer rear
body, full-length hardtop, station wagon and
County station wagon, the last with self-
levelling rear axle and power-assisted steering
as standard. Inside, the heating and ventilation
facilities were improved and, for the first time,
air conditioning was made available, leading to
the dropping of the 'safari' twin-skin roof on the
station wagon. In February 1984 the 2,286cc
diesel engine was discontinued, to be replaced
by a 67bhp 2,494cc unit.

June 1984 saw the short-wheelbase variants
given the same treatment, when the Ninety
was launched – despite the name, and the '90'
grille badge, the wheelbase was actually 92.9in
(2,360mm). Initially there was no V8 engine
option and buyers had to choose between
the 2,286cc petrol engine or the 2,494cc four-
cylinder diesel, both engines being mated to a
five-speed gearbox with permanent four-wheel

**ABOVE** Long-wheelbase Defender in communications mode. The hatch behind the driver's door conceals a space for stowing jerrycans. The yellow 'flag' across the roof is used for air recognition. *(Phil Royal)*

**LEFT** Displaying the identification mark used by the Coalition forces during the liberation of Kuwait, this short-wheelbase Defender is fitted with the standard military hardtop. *(Warehouse Collection)*

**ABOVE** The black-and-white disruptive camouflage of this long-wheelbase Defender FFR is effective against a background of snow. Note the air-recognition 'flag' on the roof, the snorkel, and the exhaust pipe extension coiled around the spare wheel. *(Phil Royal)*

drive. Like the 110, the 90 was available as a canvas- or steel-cabbed pickup truck, full-length hardtop, station wagon and County station wagon. Wind-up windows were available for the first time on both models.

The V8 engine was also offered for the 90 in May 1985, in combination with the five-speed gearbox being assembled at the Santana factory in Spain. And three months later, in August 1985, the old petrol engine was ousted in favour of an uprated 2,494cc unit with a power output of 83bhp. From October 1986 a turbocharged diesel engine was available as an option, raising the power output by 25%; this proved so popular that it wasn't long before the turbocharged diesel became the norm.

In the summer of 1985 the range had been extended by the inclusion of a stretched 4x4 variant with a 127in wheelbase, designated the '127'. This was offered with a six-seater crew cab and a shortened version of the high-capacity pickup bed, and power-assisted steering was a standard fitment. At the same time, Sandringham Motor Company (SMC) started to market a Land Rover-approved V8-powered 6x6 fitted with Range Rover axles

in a variation of the drive-line used in their Stage One-based Sandringham Six.

In 1990 the entire range was rebranded 'Defender', with the models known as the Defender 90 and the Defender 110; what would have been the Defender 127 became the Defender 130, although the wheelbase remained unchanged at 127in. At the same time the 200Tdi turbocharged diesel engine (first seen in the Discovery in 1989) was made available, giving civilian customers a choice of four engines for the Defender 90 and 110: 2,495cc four-cylinder and 3,528cc V8 petrol engines, and 2,495cc diesel engines available in naturally-aspirated and turbocharged form. The Defender 130 was available only with the V8 petrol engine or the turbocharged diesel. All three models were fitted with a five-speed gearbox, with that fitted to the V8-engined vehicles being a different design, and there was also a two-speed transfer case and the permanent four-wheel-drive system from the Range Rover, with a lockable centre differential.

By 1994 the 200Tdi engine had been upgraded and reworked to meet new European emissions regulations. Described as the

300Tdi, the new power unit had the same capacity and power output as the 200Tdi, producing 111bhp from 2,495cc, but was improved in terms of reliability, smoothness of operation, and noise and harshness. In 1998 the 300Tdi was superseded by an entirely new five-cylinder 2,493cc engine designated Td5, replaced in turn by the Puma Td4 in 2007, necessitating a distinctive bulge in the formerly flat engine cover. The Puma Td4 is a 2,402cc four-cylinder common-rail diesel with a power output of 122bhp based on the Ford/Mazda Duratorque range, and until 2012 was the only engine option for the civilian Defender. Finally, in late 2011, for the 2012 model year, the Puma engine was replaced by a four-cylinder turbocharged diesel producing the same power and torque figures as the Puma, from a capacity of 2,198cc. At the same time, the five-speed gearbox was superseded by a new six-speed unit.

Despite frequent predictions of its imminent demise – the current cut-off date being mooted as 2014 – the range remains in production into 2012 as the Defender 90, 110 and 130, in a range of body options.

**ABOVE** This unique disruptive camouflage consisting of rectangles of grey, white and terracotta, was devised by the officer commanding the 4/7 Royal Dragoon Guards tank squadron in Berlin, and was found to be effective in concealing military vehicles in urban areas where objects and shadows tend to have straight edges and the more usual green and black is inappropriate. *(Phil Royal)*

**BELOW** Now awaiting disposal, this long-wheelbase Defender has probably spent its working life as part of a REME light aid detachment recovery unit. Note the work platform on the roof. *(Warehouse Collection)*

'The Land Rover is a general-purpose passenger and load-carrying truck with accommodation for driver and five passengers. The vehicle can be driven in two-wheel or four-wheel drive as required. Some vehicles are fitted with a detachable canvas tilt and others with a hardtop.'

**Air Publication A.P.2782B**
March 1965

## Chapter Two

# Land Rover joins up

Despite its undeniable military origins, Rover had always seen the Land Rover as an essentially agricultural machine, even to the extent of ensuring that the power take-off shaft was compatible with that of the Ferguson tractor. It is commonly suggested that there was never any intention of seeking military orders, but the Rover sales office must have been well aware that the vehicle had military potential even before its launch at the Amsterdam Motor Show. In fact the first enquiry for a military Land Rover had come from the Indian Army in March 1948.

**OPPOSITE** A pair of Defender Wolf XD vehicles form part of a line of privately-owned ex-military Land Rovers. *(Phil Royal)*

ABOVE Standard 80in military Series I general service cargo vehicle. Note the two-piece military 'combat' wheels and the early (pre-1954) non-recessed door handles. The mudguard-mounted indicators have been fitted in the position normally occupied by the sidelights, and new non-matching sidelights have been fitted alongside. *(Simon Thomson)*

ABOVE The 86in and 88in Series Is were fitted with recessed door handles and stronger mounts for the side-screens. This example, in RAF service, is finished in overall blue-grey gloss paint. Note the decidedly civilian-style radio antenna and the high-level semaphore indicators. *(Warehouse Collection)*

The British War Office was equally convinced of the military potential of the Land Rover, and a pair of pre-production vehicles had ended up at the Fighting Vehicle Development Establishment's Chertsey facility in June 1948. At the time, the War Office was busy with developing its own version of the American Jeep, and it could be argued that the Land Rover was almost press-ganged into military service as a response to the development problems that were being experienced with this project.

Before the end of World War Two the War Office had begun to investigate the possibility of producing a British version of the ubiquitous Jeep, and by 1946 the plans were beginning to come to fruition in the shape of the Nuffield Mechanizations' Gutty. Designed, at least in part, by Alec Issigonis, the Gutty employed semi-stressed skin construction, a flat-four water-cooled engine and all-round independent torsion-bar suspension. By August 1948 the Gutty had metamorphosed into the FV1800 Wolseley Mudlark, and this in turn led to the production FV1801, retaining some of the features of the Gutty but, crucially, considerably more complex – and expensive – than the Jeep. In May or June 1950 Rover was invited

LEFT Lacking a hood and side-screens, this 86in Series I was photographed in Aden during the 'emergency' there in 1963–67. Note the sand tyres and rear grab handles, the latter typical of early military Land Rovers. *(IWM, ADN62-10-11)*

to tender for the FV1801 production contract, but, indicating that they were not interested, the company countered by offering the War Office the standard Land Rover. For their part, the War Office indicated that they wished to press ahead with the FV1801, and the production contract eventually went to the Austin Motor Company for the vehicle that became known as the Champ. However, difficulties experienced during trials of the Champ meant that series production did not get under way before 1951 or 1952.

At the same time, the British Army's Jeeps were not getting any younger, and with the Champ project nowhere near fruition the War Office was forced to look elsewhere for a replacement – bringing the Land Rover back into the story.

## Military trials

In an attempt to get over what was becoming a critical shortage of utility vehicles, the War Office proposed that the Jeep-like Land Rover might serve as a stopgap measure. Not only would this solve the immediate problem but, once deliveries of the Champ got under way, the Land Rover, with its similar payload and outline design, could remain in service as a 'general purpose' partner. The Ministry of Supply purchased two pre-production Land Rovers for trials: a left-hand-drive model (chassis number L29), and a right-hand-drive vehicle (R30); these were followed by a third vehicle, with the Tickford station wagon body. In June 1948 the first two vehicles were tested on the off-road courses that made up the FVDE's Chertsey proving ground. At the end of the trials a number of possible improvements were suggested, but the concluding report was generally favourable, and an additional 20 vehicles were ordered from the initial production run for 'further evaluation'.

In one of a series of monthly bulletins describing developments in new equipment, FVDE informed the user services that 'a Land Rover vehicle has been procured for trials in view of the possibility of a number of these vehicles being used by the Services as an interim measure' – in other words, until the Champ project was concluded. A year later, in

1949, G.P. Walsh, Deputy Director of Weapons Development, wrote that 'the Land Rover would meet the requirements (for the so-called utility range)... but it is considered that a Jeep with relaxed specification is required in order to maintain some standardisation... providing the

**ABOVE** Brand-new 86in or 88in Series I photographed in the Far East or Hong Kong. *(IWM, FEHK62-124-6)*

**BELOW** In 1949 a number of 80in Series Is were used as a mobile test bed for the Rolls-Royce B40 engine that was intended for the Austin Champ; the conversion required the wheelbase to be extended to 81in. Once the trials were over at least one example, as seen here, was converted to a royal review vehicle. *(Warehouse Collection)*

cost approaches that of the Land Rover'. Of course, no such Jeep was available; and worse still the cost of the FV1801 project continued to escalate as the user services made ever more demands of the vehicle.

At the end of 1949 two production Land Rovers were acquired and subjected to a second series of military trials in order to check whether or not the modifications made following the report on the pre-production machines were satisfactory. On 5 January 1950, after the first vehicle had run a little more than 10,000 miles (16,200km), a preliminary report was issued, noting a number of minor failures. The only real difficulty seemed to concern the water pump, which had given continual trouble before finally being replaced with a unit of modified design. The engine was stripped and measurements were taken of the cylinder bores, with the wear determined to be 'well within acceptable limits'. It was stated that the condition of the vehicle was 'good', comparing favourably with that of the pre-production machines, and that the modifications introduced as a result of the first series of trials 'had so far proved effective'. The trial was resumed.

The second vehicle fared rather less favourably, with the rear axle failing before 20,000 miles (32,400km) had been covered. As a result of poor setting-up of the assembly at the Rover factory, five of the crown-wheel teeth had sheared resulting in damage to the pinion. The unit was replaced and the trial continued. On 8 September 1950, A.E. Masters, FVDE Chief Engineer, issued the final report on the second vehicle, which by now had covered 20,356 miles (33,000km), of which some 4,500 (7,290km) had been cross-country. Replacements during the trials included one set of spark plugs, a water pump, gearbox selector spring, rear-axle differential, four Silentbloc bushes, a rear spring and six tyres and bump rubbers. This rate of component expenditure was considered to be 'satisfactory', but the engine was stripped for internal examination. The degree of wear suggested that engine life to first major overhaul would be in the order of 20,000 miles (32,400km) – although it is unclear whether this meant another 20,000 miles (32,400km) or whether the engine was actually already requiring an overhaul. In its final conclusion, the report stated quite categorically that 'the production type Land Rover as supplied to the Army has a satisfactory degree of reliability, especially in view of the fact that it is a standard vehicle in commercial production'.

And so began the 'civilian' Land Rover's illustrious military career – with the vehicle seeing its first combat service in Korea alongside the British Army's ageing Jeeps and, later, alongside the Austin Champ.

The Army received the first of 1,910 cargo vehicles during 1949, whilst the RAF took delivery of its first batch of 100 vehicles in May 1950. These were the first of many such contracts, covering the short-wheelbase cargo vehicle in its various guises, as well as the long-wheelbase station wagon – the latter also being modified to provide a military field ambulance. Although various contracts called for a degree of light modification to better suit the vehicle to its military service, these generally only concerned items such as wheels, and electrical and lighting equipment, and there was never any attempt made at producing an exclusively military Land Rover. Even when the War Office purchased some 675 rear-wheel-drive only station wagons in 1958, these were still derived from the standard civilian machine.

However, although it was still being stated by the War Office that there was no intention of abandoning the sophisticated Champ, which had finally entered series production in 1952, orders for the Land Rover Series I continued to be placed throughout the production life of the vehicle. By the time production came to an end in 1958 some 15,000 Series Is had been delivered to the services.

In 1956, the Wilks brothers were asked to attend a meeting at what had, by that time, become the Fighting Vehicles Research & Development Establishment (FVRDE), to discuss the future of the Land Rover in military service. The production run for the Champ had only just been completed and the War Office was maintaining the view that the two vehicles could be operated alongside one another. However, just two years later, in August 1958, the Director, Weapons Development, wrote that '40 per cent of the ¼ ton vehicles in the British Army are Land Rovers... [and that the Land Rover] has become the standard ¼ ton tactical and utility vehicle', going on to state that 'the War Office has every confidence in the Land Rover as a tactical front line vehicle'. By 1961, as the Series IIA started to enter service, the writing was very much on the wall for the Champ, and by 1966 all of the Champs had either been disposed of or passed to the Territorials.

In little more than ten years the essentially civilian Land Rover, initially purchased as an 'interim' measure, had replaced the

**ABOVE The Land Rover was initially purchased by the War Office as an interim measure pending completion of development of the FV1801 Austin Champ, seen here. Complex and expensive, the Champ had been intended as a replacement for the British Army's World War Two Jeeps, but by 1957–58 the Army had decided to standardise on the Land Rover and dispose of the Champs.** *(Warehouse Collection)*

military Champ – which, incidentally had cost the taxpayer a total of £1,130–1,200 per vehicle, without even considering the cost of development, when the price of a Series I Land Rover to the Ministry of Supply was in the order of £450–600, with no development costs at all!

All three of the British armed services operated Land Rovers in large numbers. Series I and II vehicles were acquired by both the War Office and the Air Ministry, the latter on behalf of the Royal Air Force, who actually took the

**LEFT Introduced in April 1958, the Series II can easily be identified by the increased width of the body. This example entered service July 1960.**
*(RAWHS)*

largest share of the military Series IIs. Smaller numbers were acquired by the Admiralty for the Royal Navy. Despite a period of neglect in the late 1980s and early 1990s that led to a critical situation with the Army's Land Rover fleet, Series IIA, Series III and Defender vehicles continued to be operated by all three services. The 'lightweight' was used only by the Army and the RAF, and the strictly-military 'Wolf' XD remains in service only with the Army.

But the Land Rover's military successes were not confined to Britain. In the same way that civilian export sales had been brisk from the outset, it wasn't long before other nations started to see the Land Rover as a low-cost, no-nonsense utility vehicle. There was also a degree of interest from overseas in the possibilities of assembling the vehicle locally, and as early as November 1949 Rover had entered discussions with the French company Talbot-Darracq about the possibility of licensing the Land Rover for construction in France. Like the British Army, the French were looking at how their ageing American Jeeps might be replaced, and the Land Rover seemed to fit the bill perfectly. Sadly there was no satisfactory conclusion to the talks, and the French Army ended up buying the Delahaye VLR-D, before abandoning this in favour of the licence-built Jeep M201 from Hotchkiss. However, by 1951 the Belgian company Minerva had secured a licence to build the Land Rover, supplying their particular take on the Series I theme to the Belgian Army and Gendarmerie from 1952, whilst in 1952–53 a similar vehicle was constructed in West Germany by Tempo for the *Bundesgrenzschutz* border guards.

Ultimately Land Rovers were licensed for construction or assembly from completely knocked-down (CKD) kits in Australia, Belgium, Brazil, Kenya, Malaysia, Morocco, New Zealand, Nigeria, Trinidad, Turkey, Spain, West Germany, Zaire, Zambia and Zimbabwe.

## Military modifications

With few exceptions, the military Land Rover is little different from its civilian counterpart. For example, for the Series I and II typical military modifications were often no more elaborate than the use of standardised

ABOVE Standard 88in Series II general service cargo vehicle. One of a huge number of long- and short-wheelbase vehicles supplied under contract KL/H/01305, this particular example started life assigned to the Army Driving School. *(Warehouse Collection)*

RIGHT The Series III, introduced in September 1971, can be identified by the plastic moulded grille that replaced the original wire mesh pattern. This example, in private hands, is a long-wheelbase communications vehicle. *(Phil Royal)*

military-style lighting equipment, the addition of a NATO-style towing pintle, and split-rim wheels shod with aggressive bar-grip pattern tyres. Some Series IIA vehicles had strengthened axles, military-pattern double-height 'pusher' bumpers, twin fuel tanks and split-rim 'combat' wheels – but none of these modifications were applied to all of the vehicles procured. One military version that had no civilian counterpart was the unique Series I and Series II vehicles that were converted to a 4x2 driveline by locking the transfer box in the 'high' range and fitting a simple tubular front axle to which the standard swivel housings were attached. These vehicles were purchased in the late 1950s and were described as 'utility cars', with the War Office stating that they were intended for 'administrative use' only.

For the Series III, military-pattern vehicles could be identified by the special rear cross-member, NATO towing pintle, 'pusher' bumpers, and lashing rings and tie-down loops in the cargo area; twin 45-litre fuel tanks were placed under the front seats. There was also provision for stowing a water jerrycan up against the rear bulkhead; rifle clips were fitted

to the bulkhead, and clips were provided on the tailgate for pioneer tools. Optional equipment included a front-mounted 5,000lb (2,273kg) mechanical drum winch or a 3,000lb (1,364kg) capstan winch, and Aeon rubber helper springs.

Although most of the Series II, IIA and III vehicles supplied to the British Army were petrol-engined, diesel power was occasionally specified where there was undue fire risk. Other users

ABOVE Hardtop-equipped Series III dating from 1977, awaiting sale to a new owner. Note how the matt military paint finish behaves when subjected to prolonged weathering. *(Ian Young)*

ABOVE The blackout light and the indicators mounted on the mudguard tops identify these Series III vehicles as having served with the Royal Netherlands Army. *(Warehouse Collection)*

ABOVE RIGHT Photographed in the United Arab Emirates in 2011, this Omani Series III is equipped for the communications role. Note the wooden supports stowed behind the front bumper, presumably to allow a simple shelter to be attached to the vehicle. *(Simon Thomson)*

BELOW Long-wheelbase Series III marked as a Military Police vehicle. *(Phil Royal)*

were less squeamish about diesel engines, and in 1978, for example, the Royal Danish Army was supplied with what was essentially a commercial Series III fitted with a 2,286cc diesel engine, with either 12V or 24V electrical systems.

The so-called 'core military' Defender was, of course, offered with a choice of engines, and was the first diesel-engined Land Rover to be purchased by the British Army in significant numbers. There was also a choice of a 12V or 24V electrical system, using either a 65Ah or

120Ah alternator for the 12V vehicles or single or twin 50Ah alternators for the 24V vehicles. Optional equipment included stowage facilities for jerrycans (long-wheelbase vehicles), rollover protection, vision panels in the hood sides, full-length hardtop, NATO inter-vehicle starting socket, lashing cleats in the rear cargo area, 12-pin NATO trailer socket, JATE air-lifting and lashing rings, and a spare wheel mounting on either the side of the body or on the engine cover. On the Defender platform, Land Rover has also shown what was described as the 'Defender 110 utility station wagon', intended for use as an operational logistics reconnaissance vehicle, and the 'Defender 110 hardtop' in so-called 'fitted for radio' (FFR) form. The station wagon was equipped with a four-door body with three rows of seats, and was fitted with a radio table, roof rack and external ladder. The 'Defender 110 hardtop' could be specified with either a standard or glass-reinforced composite plastic (GRP) top,

**ABOVE LEFT** Long-wheelbase Series III of the Royal Netherlands Army. Note the oversized brush guard and transparent area in the side curtains. *(Ian Young)*

**ABOVE RIGHT** Standard long-wheelbase Series III general service cargo vehicle showing the typical British Army green and black disruptive camouflage pattern. *(Phil Royal)*

**LEFT** Introduced at the Geneva Motor Show in 1983, the Defender is easily identified by its flush radiator grille, and was the first Land Rover to feature coil-spring suspension. The short-wheelbase variant that followed in 1984, seen here in the communications role, was described as the Defender Ninety... but was badged 'Defender 90'. *(Phil Royal)*

and was also fitted with a radio table, as well as forward-facing seating for the radio operator. Both vehicles were powered by the standard 2.4-litre diesel engine.

## Communications

One area where the military Land Rover differs significantly from its civilian counterpart is in those vehicles intended for the communications role – designated 'FFR' or 'fitted for radio'. Military communications equipment tends to place considerably more onerous demands on the vehicle's electrical system than anything used in the civilian sphere, calling for additional electrical components and facilities required

**ABOVE** Photographed in January 2010, a US airman guides a Latvian Army special operations Defender 110 into an MC-130H Combat Talon 2 aircraft in Rukla, Lithuania. Note the bumper-mounted winch. *(US DoD, Isaac A. Graham)*

**RIGHT CENTRE** Line-up of British Army Defenders awaiting disposal. *(Ian Young)*

**RIGHT** Defender 110 marked as a communications vehicle, from the liberation of Kuwait. *(Phil Royal)*

**ABOVE** Although the hardtop Defender 110 was widely used in the communications role, this example has been fitted with a roof-top working platform. *(Ian Young)*

**RIGHT** Defender 90 communications vehicle. *(Ian Young)*

**BELOW RIGHT** Looking decidedly the worse for wear, this Defender 90 communications vehicle is unusual in having been equipped with a substantial roll-over protection system (ROPS). *(Ian Young)*

to support and connect the radios, as well as screening and shielding equipment.

In the Series I these modifications consisted of little more than a pair of additional batteries in the rear compartment designed to power the radio equipment, a radio table, screened ignition components, junction boxes and antenna mounts. By the time the Series II, IIA and III vehicles entered service the electrical system for FFR vehicles had been upgraded to 24V and the dynamo replaced by a 100Ah alternator; this allowed the supplementary batteries to be coupled into the vehicle's electrical system and float-charged while the engine was running, the state of charge being indicated by ammeters on the instrument panel.

Things had got considerably more serious by the time the Defender had appeared, and the 'core military' offering was available with a choice of single or twin 24V 50Ah alternators,

bonding leads and radio suppression equipment, and radio-screened heater and windscreen wiper motors. For the FFR role, users could further specify additional 12V batteries, a radio table in the rear, racking on the roll bar, separate radio operator's seats, antenna and tuner mountings on the tops of the front mudguards, antenna mounting brackets at the rear, antenna cables, outlets for antenna cables in the hood, connection box with ammeter, and a hand throttle on the right-hand side of the dash.

## Midlife rebuild

From 2007, the British Army started to extend the service careers of the remaining 1,000 or so standard Defenders by means of a midlife rebuild dubbed 'Project Tithonus'. Managed by the Defence Equipment & Support's 'Light Utility Vehicle Team', the rebuild process provides significant improvements in user safety, with a full roll-over protection system, improved seating, and noise- and vibration-reducing matting. Other improvements include an under-body protection coating and an overhauled braking system.

Similarly, 'Project Remus', first shown to the public in 2010, is a safety and legislative-compliance upgrade for the more recent long-wheelbase Wolf XD Defender. Upgrades included a front roll-over protection system, inertia seatbelts at the rear and acoustic matting to the cab and rear areas.

Also dating from 2010, 'Project Hebe' is a feasibility prototype constructed on the 127/130in chassis of the Pulse battlefield ambulance. The vehicle was fitted with a hardtop four-man crew cab with a raised roof constructed by Broadwater Mouldings; the cab area included a distinctive raised-roof to accommodate a Safety Devices International rollover protection system, and there was a 1,750–2,200lb (800–1,000kg) capacity

**LEFT** Dating from 2007, 'Project Tithonus' was a British Army midlife rebuild programme designed to extend the service lives of the remaining Defenders. The rebuild process includes a full roll-over protection system, improved seating, and noise- and vibration-reducing matting. (Warehouse Collection)

pickup body with a drop tailgate. Since the prototype was based on the Wolf XD running gear, the power unit was the standard military specification 2.5-litre 300Tdi, driving through a five-speed gearbox. Suggested roles include convoy escort vehicle or mortar carrier, the latter as a replacement for the obsolete Reynolds-Boughton RB44. It was said that up to 300 vehicles could be available for conversion from 2015, and that this could extend the service life of the Wolf fleet to 2030!

Land Rover have also developed a similar machine described as the 'Defender 130 double cabin high-capacity pickup'. Like 'Hebe', this also featured an enclosed four-man cab and high-capacity pickup body, but in this instance based on the standard 'core military' Defender and powered by the 2.4-litre common-rail diesel engine, in conjunction with a six-speed manual transmission.

## The future of the military Land Rover

The British Army's love affair with the Land Rover has endured for more than 60 years, and the vehicle has also seen valiant service elsewhere. However, it is widely believed in industry circles that the Defender will be unable to meet the Euro VI emission standards that come into effect in January 2014, and although it could feasibly remain in production overseas, and simply not be made available in European markets, clearly some replacement will be required.

It is hard to imagine worldwide military customers queuing up to buy the recently announced (2011) Land Rover DC100 concept vehicle that has been mooted as the Defender replacement, and we may be witnessing the end of the conventional military Land Rover.

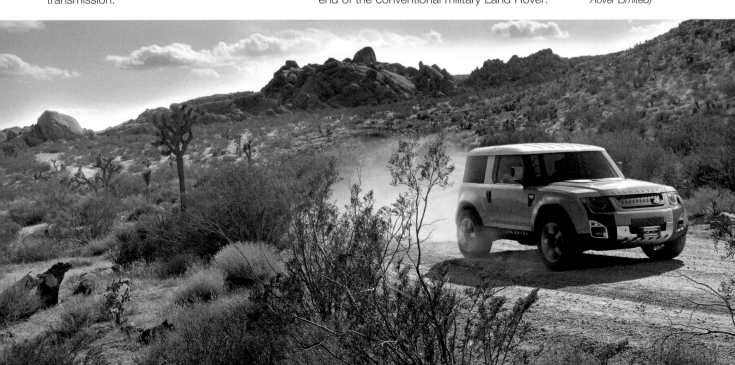

*"The vehicle must be capable of floating, when fully laden, in inland waters. It is acceptable that this is achieved by use of a flotation kit. This kit need not be stowed on the vehicle but must be capable of being fitted quickly by the driver and one passenger.'*

**The War Office; 'Military characteristics for the Truck Airportable General Purpose'**
June 1962

## Chapter Three

# Purpose-built military vehicles

When considering the early Series I, II and III models, it is slightly misleading to talk about 'military Land Rovers' since most actually differed little from their civilian counterparts. Whilst small modifications were made to equip these vehicles for a life of military abuse, any specialised military Land Rovers of the period tended to be constructed by army workshops, or by a third party. It wasn't until the appearance of the 'lightweight', the forward-control '101' and the Wolf Defender that Land Rover could be said to have produced a purpose-designed military vehicle.

**OPPOSITE** Following the amphibious landings that contributed so much to the success of the Allied invasion of Europe in 1944, NATO became obsessed with developing vehicles that had innate wading capabilities. One such was the FV18051 air-portable general purpose (APGP) Land Rover. *(IWM, MVE48368-9)*

Had the Land Rover been designed from the outset as a purely military vehicle it would almost certainly have fallen victim to the same schools of thought that had resulted in the Champ being unnecessarily complex, over-engineered, overweight and over-priced – a military Champ cost some two and a half times more than a civilian Land Rover for what was arguably a similar standard of performance and capacity. Admittedly, the Champ featured waterproofed and radio-screened electrical equipment, built-in wading capability, high-speed cross-country performance and the ability to travel fast using five reverse gears. The Land Rover could pull off none of these tricks, but for most of the time this level of performance was simply redundant.

It was the imperatives of the civilian market that kept the price of the Solihull product down to a reasonable level and the technical complexity to a minimum, and the key to the success of the Land Rover, as a military vehicle, lies in its adaptability and in the economies of scale available from mass production.

Nevertheless, over the years the factory has produced vehicles such as the Series IIA 'lightweight', the forward-control 1-tonne '101' and the Wolf Defender XD, all of which should be considered to be purpose-made military vehicles, even if, in practice, they were still heavily-modified versions of the standard civilian offering.

# Air-portable general service (APGP)

### APGP 'Scheme A'

The amphibious landings that had contributed to the success of the invasion of Europe in 1944 had left the military with an obsession for vehicles that could float and swim, and in the late 1950s the Fighting Vehicles Research & Development Establishment began to look at ways of making standard soft-skin vehicles swim. Trials were carried out on vehicles fitted with rubber buoyancy bags inflated by the engine exhaust – one such trial mounted a Series I on a steel frame inside an oval rubber pontoon, but the result was unnecessarily cumbersome and it was decided to attach the buoyancy aids to the vehicle, rather than the

other way round. By the early 1960s, the need for an air-portable amphibious vehicle saw this technique applied to a hybrid Series II vehicle that was described as 'FV18051, truck, air-portable, general purpose (APGP), Scheme A'.

In June 1962 a document was produced describing the 'military characteristics' of the vehicle, and stating that 'a requirement exists for a vehicle which can be carried in transport aircraft in numbers which make the fullest use of the payload of the aircraft... this vehicle must fulfil most of the vehicle roles until the arrival of the sea tail and must enable combat and support units to move freely across country and water obstacles with only limited engineer support'. The document went on to describe how 'a new special truck is required' that was to incorporate 'as many standard Land Rover components and assemblies as possible, compatible with fulfilling its operational role'. The vehicle was required to be 'both simple and robust', with minimum practical kerb weight and a payload-to-weight ratio that would exceed existing vehicles. Cross-country performance was to be 'better than existing GS vehicles in the equivalent range', and the vehicle was to be capable of floating, fully-laden, on inland waters, probably by means of an *appliqué* flotation kit, which 'need not be stowed on the vehicle but must be capable of being quickly fitted by the driver and one passenger'. With the kit in place, 'approach and departure angles were to be equal to, or better than the existing Series II vehicles' and, without the kit, the vehicle was to be 'capable of negotiating the ramps of aircraft, landing ships, and landing craft'.

Ideally, the War Office would have preferred the vehicle to be powered by a multi-fuel diesel engine – a power unit that could run with almost equal efficiency on diesel, petrol, kerosene, aviation spirit or jet fuel. Several manufacturers were working on engines of this type, including Rover, who had been talking to the War Office about such a power unit since 1956, but none had reached fruition. A petrol engine was said to be acceptable 'as an interim measure', but the operating range across country was to be 300 miles (486km) with the multi-fuel engine, or 240 miles (389km) for the petrol engine.

The standard open-topped style of body was considered acceptable, but side-screens and a top were required to protect the crew, and a removable hardtop was required to allow the vehicle to be used in computer, missile- and fuse-test roles, and as a communications vehicle. The specification also called for a penthouse to allow conversion to the command or office role, plus removable tubular frames to accept two or possibly three stretchers. Typical weapons would include the general-purpose machine gun (GPMG), WOMBAT anti-tank gun, or medium-range anti-tank guided weapon system, and the vehicle was to be suitable for towing a trailer, 105mm pack howitzer or other wheeled equipment up to 50 per cent of its gross weight. Finally, the air-portability requirement stated that the 'maximum practical number of vehicles' were to be fitted into an Argosy, Avro 748 MF or Beverley aircraft. Stacking of empty vehicles was permitted, but there was to be a minimum of dismantling, since the vehicles were required to be operational 'within one hour of landing'. The fully-loaded vehicle was also to be capable of making airborne parachute and assault landings, from a medium stressed parachute platform.

Land Rover engineers Mike Broadhead and Norman Busby based the design of the APGP on a heavily modified long-wheelbase (109in) Series II powered by the standard 2,286cc four-cylinder engine. A lower-ratio rear axle was fitted and the vehicle was rated for a 1-ton payload, rather than the normal ¾-ton. Three prototypes were constructed, one of which was shown at the exhibition of military vehicles at FVRDE's Chertsey site in 1962.

The low-sided body was widened aft of the scuttle, shortened at the rear, and lacked doors and a tailgate. There were folding seats in the rear, but these were not carried across to the production vehicles, which were equipped instead with removable squabs and side rails. A flat-packed hardtop could be fitted for the test or communications role, and a large penthouse tent was normally carried on the roof, which could be erected to one side to enable the vehicle to be used as a command post or wireless station. With the rear seats folded flat, or the side rails removed, the vehicles could be carried, stacked two (or three) high, in a transport aircraft by removing the front wheels of the second vehicle and placing it on top of the first, with the two bodies facing in

**LEFT** One of three prototypes constructed for the amphibious air-portable general purpose (APGP Scheme A) project in 1962. Rated at 1 ton, and designed by Mike Broadhead and Norman Busby, the vehicle was based on a heavily modified long-wheelbase (109in) Series II. *(Tank Museum)*

**LEFT** Flotation bags were attached to the perimeter of the body to allow the APGP to float; propulsion in the water was provided by the wheels and by a small propeller on the rear driveshaft. *(Warehouse Collection)*

**BELOW** APGP with inflated bags attached to the side frames. *(Warehouse Collection)*

less than 1½mph (2.5kph). The propeller could be removed and replaced by a spacer to reduce drag on the road.

Initial trials were completed by 7 June 1962, when a contract was issued for 12 vehicles; this was extended in October 1964 to cover another eight, this time fitted with winches. Land Rover records suggest that 28 vehicles were actually built, although only 20 entered military service. By the time the vehicle entered production the Series II had been replaced by the Series IIA, and this was used as the basis for the production vehicles. The flotation bags – some of which were round, others oval – were produced by Avon Rubber, reputedly at lower cost, and were supported on curved rather than straight arms. Some contemporary photographs show the vehicles to be fitted with four bags, at the front and rear and along each side, others show three bags, only at the sides and rear. Other changes included the use of the standard military double-height 'pusher' bumpers at front and rear, and the eventual removal of the step rails that had formed simple sills on the prototype.

The vehicles were issued for troop trials during 1963–64, but were never adopted or produced in greater quantity, effectively being superseded by the air-portable 'lightweight' in 1968.

### APGP 'Scheme B'

A second amphibious Land Rover – 'FV18061, truck, air-portable, general purpose (APGP),

**ABOVE With flotation bags attached front and rear and along both sides, one of the prototype APGPs gingerly enters the Chertsey wading tank.** *(IWM, MVE48368-1)*

opposite directions. The upper vehicle was held in place by a cradle, and its suspension was compressed to reduce the total height.

To aid buoyancy, the chassis cavities were filled with foam and the early prototypes were actually able to float unaided, with around an inch (25mm) of freeboard, but an *appliqué* flotation kit was essential. For the prototypes the kit was developed by RFD Limited, and consisted of a pair of oval-shaped rubberised-canvas buoyancy bags on removable tubular alloy frames along the sides and rear of the vehicle. The bags were inflated from the vehicle's exhaust, and when not in use could be folded away and stowed in compartments under the rear floor. There was no rudder and the wheels were used to provide both directional control and propulsion in the water. Additional thrust came from a small three-bladed propeller on the rear propeller shaft, but unfortunately it was too close to the differential, meaning that the top speed in the water was

**BELOW On dry land the APGP was able to act as a tractor for the Italian-made 105mm Model 56 (L5) pack howitzer that entered service in 1957.** *(Tank Museum)*

**BELOW Artist's impression of the air-portable general purpose 'Scheme B'. It was an advanced exoskeleton design using foamed reinforced plastic with load-bearing steel, and although a single prototype was constructed there was no series production.** *(Warehouse Collection)*

Scheme B' – was mooted, but never progressed beyond the mock-up stage. Employing standard Series II automotive components, with the same transfer case as that used on 'Scheme A', the conventional chassis frame was replaced by an exoskeleton body of foamed reinforced plastic, with load-bearing steel inserts carrying the engine, transmission and axles. The wheelbase was 97in, and the unladen weight was 3,500lb (1,591kg).

An artist's impression of the machine appeared in the 1962 FVRDE exhibition catalogue, showing a sleek, futuristic forward-control vehicle, and by the following year this had been translated into a clumsy engineering model. This was subsequently demonstrated at FVRDE, but nothing came of the project.

**LEFT** Dating from 1965, this is the first prototype for the ½-ton 'lightweight', shown in its built-up form. *(Tank Museum)*

## Series IIA and III 'lightweight'

Although officially designated 'truck, ½ ton, GS, 4x4; Rover 1, FV18101' (*et seq*), enthusiasts usually describe the vehicle as the 'lightweight' – not because it is especially light, but because it has been designed to be readily stripped for air-portability whilst remaining fully operational. In stripped form the unladen weight reduces to around 2,660lb (1,209kg), compared to 3,322lb (1,510kg) for the standard 88in Series IIA.

The idea of producing an air-portable vehicle capable of carrying a useful military payload, and of towing a support weapon or supply trailer, dated from the latter stages of World War Two, when strategists advocated the fast deployment of troops and equipment by air. The standard British utility vehicle at this time was the Jeep, but it was too heavy for air-portability without being heavily modified. In time the Jeep was replaced by the Champ and the Land Rover Series I, both of which were also too heavy for delivery by air. By 1961 the Series I had started to be superseded by the Series II, but with an unladen weight of 3,146lb (1,430kg) it was still too heavy for air-portability and experiments continued in other directions, the Army even toying with the Mini-Moke as a possible air-portable machine.

Clearly, what was really needed was a standard utility vehicle that could be easily delivered by air, but the War Office was on record as stating that 'the current WD short-wheelbase Land Rover is too wide and too heavy' for certain air-portable roles. Nevertheless, with thousands in service the authorities were reluctant to abandon the benefits of standardisation and there was little real enthusiasm for buying a completely different vehicle for the air-portable role. The obvious answer was to reduce the weight of the Land Rover, and in 1964 a specification was issued for what was described as a 'lightweight version of the short wheelbase Land Rover' that could be carried by Argosy, Beverley and Britannia aircraft, or slung beneath a Wessex heavy-lift helicopter.

A written specification called for a maximum overall width of 60in (1,524mm) to allow two vehicles to be carried in the width of an Argosy fuselage, and an unladen weight that was not to exceed 2,500lb (1,136kg) for the 12V cargo variant, and 3,100lb (1,409kg) for the 24V FFR version. The range was to be a minimum of 300 miles (486km), and the vehicle was to be capable of carrying a payload of 1,000lb (455kg) including the driver, and of towing a 10cwt (500kg) trailer. However, the Series IIA (Rover 8) would have had to shed around 500lb (227kg) to be capable of fulfilling the role as defined. And, what's more, all of the weight saving would have to be made in the bodywork, since in order to simplify parts stockholding the War Office demanded that the engine, gearbox, axles, suspension and steering components were to be identical to the standard vehicle.

Undaunted, Mike Broadhead and Norman

Busby set to work on designing such a vehicle with assistance from FVRDE and, subsequently, their successors, the Military Vehicles and Engineering Establishment (MVEE). Before the project was completed, Mike Broadhead's role as project manager was handed to Bob Seager, but nevertheless, the team had the first prototype ready for testing in 1965.

Based on the standard short-wheelbase chassis, the prototype 'lightweight' was modified by the addition of a brace across the main members at the front that allowed the (narrower) front bumper to be removed: additional chassis bracing reduced flexing when the vehicle was used in this condition. The engine cover was deeper and more angular than the civilian item and, by reducing the overall width from 64in (1,626mm) to the specified 60in (1,524mm), the designers had been forced to devise a new bulkhead. Lacking a windscreen, doors, rear seat, hood and frame, and the normal body panels, the vehicle was little more than a flat platform with an engine compartment up front, seats for the crew, and raised wheel arches either side of a flat load platform. Where weight was unimportant the vehicle could be built-up to suit the role or mission, using a standard kit of parts that included a canvas hood and frame, the standard style of windscreen, flat metal doors, standard door tops, simple side panels for the rear body and a folding tailgate. From about 1969 a number of vehicles were retro-fitted with factory-style hardtops.

Power came from the standard 2,286cc petrol engine, with the oil cooler omitted to save weight. Similarly, the standard gearbox and steering components of the Series IIA were also used. The heavy-duty military suspension of the 'Rover 8' was ousted in favour of the standard civilian springs, and whilst the axles were generally identical to the production items the narrower track meant that the halfshafts were shorter, and the drive flanges were redesigned to reduce the overall width. Tyres were 6.00-16 rather than the standard military 6.50-16, mounted on one-piece commercial-type rims.

Six pre-production machines were constructed in 1966 and submitted for automotive trials at FVRDE. With the trials successfully completed, the initial production requirement was identified as being just 75 vehicles for the Royal Marines, with manufacturing scheduled to start at the end of 1967. One of the production vehicles was exhibited at the Commercial Motor Show in September 1968 – detail differences when compared to the prototype and pre-production vehicles included the reinstatement of the engine oil cooler and the use of three, rather than four, straps to secure the spare wheel to the engine cover. By the end of 1968 some 750 vehicles had been constructed, and by 1972 the 'lightweight' had been adopted as the replacement for the standard 88in Land Rover (Rover 10) in the British Army.

By the time production had started

**LEFT Production Series IIA 'lightweight'. One of a batch from contract WV7478 that started to enter service in 1969.** *(RAWHS)*

**BELOW Rear view of the production 'lightweight' in its built-up form.** *(Tank Museum)*

the payload for the 'lightweight' had been increased from ¼ ton to ½ ton, with the official designation now being 'truck, GS (or FFR), ½ ton, 4x4, Rover Mk 1'; the 12V general service (GS) machine was numbered FV18101, whilst the 24V FFR vehicle was FV18102. Aside from the use of a radio-screened 24V electrical system, the major difference between the two versions was that the FFR variant had only two front seats, the centre seat being replaced by a large battery box. A unitary radio-station mount was also designed especially for the 'lightweight'.

Production of the Series IIA-based 'lightweight' continued until March 1972, with around 3,000 vehicles produced, in both left- and right-hand-drive form. In October 1971 the standard Series IIA had been replaced by the Series III, and this change was reflected in the 'lightweight' production line when a Series III-based machine was introduced in May 1972. There was a new synchromesh gearbox, new clutch, servo-assisted brakes and a 12V alternator to replace the old DC generator, although the 24V FFR machines had always been fitted with an alternator. On late production vehicles the standard halfshafts and drive flanges were used, since the loading width was no longer deemed to be critical.

At about this time the War Office stopped assigning its own 'mark' numbers to Land Rovers and the nomenclature became 'truck, utility [or 'utility FFR'], ½ ton, 4x4, Rover Series 3', with the two variants numbered FV18103 and FV18104 respectively. The ½-ton Series 3 replaced existing 'Rover 8' and '10' machines in the British Army, with nearly 11,000 examples constructed before the line was closed in 1984. Workshop conversions were made to small numbers of vehicles to cover the ambulance, WOMBAT anti-tank, 81mm mortar and line-laying roles. British Army vehicles used in Northern Ireland were frequently fitted with *appliqué* composite GRP and Makrolon ballistic-protection panels, described as the 'Northern Ireland protection kit', and there were experiments with the use of flotation blocks designed to provide an amphibious capability. Series 3 'lightweights' were also purchased by Algeria, Belgium, Brunei, Croatia, Denmark, Egypt, Guyana, Hong Kong, Indonesia, Iran,

Jamaica, Libya, Morocco, Oman, Portugal, Saudi Arabia, Sudan and the Netherlands, the last choosing to specify a diesel engine. Ex-Dutch forces vehicles were also acquired by Croatia and Slovenia. An anti-tank variant, mounting the American M40A1 106mm recoilless rifle, was produced by Marshalls of Cambridge and was sold to the Netherlands, Oman and Saudi Arabia (see page 65).

By the late 1980s the advent of larger transport aircraft and more powerful heavy-lift helicopters made the 'lightweight' obsolete and the vehicle was eventually superseded by the Defender 90. The Netherlands Army disposed of most of its 'lightweights' during the period 1992–93, and the last examples were discharged from the British Army towards the end of the 1990s.

**ABOVE** Following trials held in 1972, the Royal Netherlands Army took delivery of both petrol- and diesel-powered Series III 'lightweights' from 1976 onwards. 'Lightweights' were also supplied to some 20 other countries. *(Ian Young)*

**BELOW** The ex-military 'lightweight' has proved popular with private owners looking for something a little different. *(Ian Young)*

RIGHT Plywood mock-up of what eventually became the 1-tonne forward-control (101 FC), produced for stowage trials. (Tank Museum)

## 1-tonne forward control

During the 1960s the War Office identified what was described as a 'serious gap in the future vehicle range between the Land Rover, with a capacity of ½ to ¾ ton, and the 4-ton Bedford MK/MJ trucks'. There was a specific and immediate requirement for a heli-portable artillery tractor for the 105mm light gun that had replaced the pack howitzer, which was too heavy to be towed by existing Land Rovers. It was also being said that 'there are many roles for which the smaller vehicles are inadequate and the larger one expensive or tactically unacceptable'.

Following a series of false starts, work on a vehicle designed to bridge this gap started in 1967, with Rover constructing five general service (GS) 1-ton military prototypes in conjunction with FVRDE. The first of these was completed by 1969, and although it generally resembled the production vehicle in most

BELOW In its first incarnation, the 1-tonne forward-control was powered by a six-cylinder 2,995cc engine, necessitating a short forward projection from the bulkhead to enclose the engine. (Tank Museum)

respects one major difference was the short 'boxy' engine compartment projection that housed the 2,995cc straight-six engine of the Rover P5. There was part-time four-wheel drive, and the vehicle rode on the heavy-duty ENV axles and differentials of the Series IIB civilian forward-control chassis.

Although it proved to be underpowered when towing a gun or loaded trailer the prototype helped to crystallise the brief, and in June 1968 a General Statement of Requirements (GSR3463) was issued that described a 1-tonne gun tractor. Other possible roles included command post, Rapier and MILAN missile launcher, missile test/repair vehicle, signals office, radio repair vehicle, computer exchange unit, dry-air generator, power-supply vehicle, battery-charging truck, line layer, load carrier and battlefield ambulance. In addition, the specification stated that the vehicle should be capable of towing a load of up to 3,300lb (1,500kg) in a powered-axle trailer, with the axle coupled to the tractor via a power take-off at the rear. It was also suggested that the truck might be used as a mount for the EMI Cymbeline mortar-locating radar system, and as a Royal Electrical & Mechanical Engineers (REME) welding shop; these roles were eventually withdrawn.

It was never a foregone conclusion that Land Rover would be awarded the contract, and the specification was presented to some 16 different motor companies in August 1968, with

invitations to tender. Vehicles considered for the role included the American M561 Condec 6x6 'Gama Goat', the Volvo-Ailsa 4140 series Laplander, and the Steyr-Puch 4x4 Pinzgauer 710, as well as vehicles from Austin, Chrysler, International, Kaiser-Jeep, Toyota and Volvo. However, the Laplander and the Land Rover were the only serious contenders.

Rover reworked their original prototype, with the resulting vehicle described as the '1-tonne forward-control Land Rover, FV19000 series'. It was rarely referred to as such, however, being more commonly described as 'forward control 101' or '101 FC', the designation being derived from the wheelbase dimension. Ten prototypes were constructed during 1970, at a total cost of £35,000. Six went to FVRDE, where they were subjected to arctic and tropical trials, whilst the remainder were intended for user trials, with three going to the School of Artillery for trials with the 105mm gun. Mock-ups were also produced which allowed concurrent development of the various equipment and installations. The trials were scheduled to end in early 1972, with the winning vehicle going into production immediately.

The vehicle was totally unlike anything the company had offered before, borrowing little from existing models. The chassis was completely new, as was the stark forward-control body. The urgency of the requirement had ruled out the use of either diesel or multi-fuel engines but, equally, FVRDE decided that

there was no suitable power unit already in service. Rover had intended to use the Buick-derived V8 destined for the Range Rover, but initially these engines were in such short supply that a 3-litre, six-cylinder Ford Falcon petrol engine was used for development work. The Range Rover gearbox and its permanent four-wheel-drive transfer case, using a lower ratio low gear, were married to heavy-duty Salisbury axles incorporating larger halfshafts than normal; an inter-axle differential lock was also fitted. There were live axles front and rear on semi-elliptical tapered multi-leaf springs, an anti-roll bar at the front and double-acting telescopic hydraulic shock absorbers all round. Approach and departure angles were excellent, and the low axle ratios (5.57:1), combined with the lower gear of the transfer box, gave a 74:1 low gear, almost twice the figure of the standard Land Rover. On the road the vehicle was capable of 79mph (128kph).

Like the ½-ton 'lightweight', demountable body panels enabled the gross vehicle weight to be reduced, in this case to 7,700lb (3,500kg), allowing it to be lifted by Wessex helicopters. The truck was also light enough to be carried in Andover or Britannia aircraft.

Examples of the matching trailer were produced by Rubery Owen and Scottorn, but the concept was not continued into production for two reasons. Firstly, because FVRDE discovered that the trailer could force the vehicle to jack-knife on tight downhill corners; and secondly – and

**LEFT The '101 FC' was first seen by the public at the 1972 Commercial Motor Show, with the first of 2,300 vehicles entering service in late 1975. This press photograph shows the vehicle coupled to the powered trailer that would have been produced by Rubery Owen or Scottorn.**

*(British Leyland plc)*

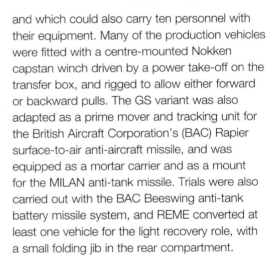

perhaps more importantly – because the trailer could only be used with one vehicle type, and this was not considered to be cost-effective.

Rover exhibited the '101 FC' at the 1972 Commercial Motor Show, with the first of 2,300 vehicles for the British Army entering service in late 1975. Production continued to 1978 when the line was shut down, but it has been suggested that the British Army might have bought 2,000 more over a period of ten years if Rover had been willing to continue producing at such a low level. There were eventually four variants, of which the most numerous (2,129 vehicles) was the general service cargo vehicle that served as a tractor for the 105mm light gun

and which could also carry ten personnel with their equipment. Many of the production vehicles were fitted with a centre-mounted Nokken capstan winch driven by a power take-off on the transfer box, and rigged to allow either forward or backward pulls. The GS variant was also adapted as a prime mover and tracking unit for the British Aircraft Corporation's (BAC) Rapier surface-to-air anti-aircraft missile, and was equipped as a mortar carrier and as a mount for the MILAN anti-tank missile. Trials were also carried out with the BAC Beeswing anti-tank battery missile system, and REME converted at least one vehicle for the light recovery role, with a small folding jib in the rear compartment.

Alongside the cargo vehicle there were 520 field ambulances (see page 61), of which 127 went to the RAF, and two types of fully-enclosed electronics/communications vehicles, all of which were constructed by modifying cargo vehicles after production. A similar body to that fitted to the ambulance – known as the 'box utility' – was designed by Lairds of Anglesey for a signals and electronics repair variant. A number of these signals vehicles were converted to biological agent detection vans

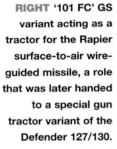

during the liberation of Kuwait. A second signals body variant, known as Vampire, was used as a signal-detection vehicle, and can be readily identified by its single side door and differently-shaped roof that accommodates a large fold-away antenna; there was also no door at the rear. Somewhere between nine and eighteen examples of this variant were constructed by Marshalls of Cambridge, with the trucks generally operating in teams of three to detect enemy radio signals by triangulation.

The total number of vehicles constructed eventually reached 2,669, with additional contracts coming from Australia, Egypt, Iran and Luxembourg.

# Defender 127/130 gun tractor

The British Aircraft Corporation (BAC) Rapier surface-to-air missile was developed for the British Army and Royal Air Force and entered service in 1971, eventually replacing other types of British surface anti-aircraft weapon, and also seeing service with the US and other armies. Two versions of the Rapier are in use in Britain:

the 'tracked Rapier', which is mounted on an American M548 tracked carrier chassis, and the 'towed Rapier', which consists of a two-wheeled launch trailer carrying four missiles. In both cases the launcher includes a cylindrical electronics module with a surveillance radar dish and 'identification friend or foe' (IFF) system under a curved radome, a guidance computer and radar transmitter, a generator, the receiver electronics, and a parabolic antenna for sending commands to the missiles. The Rapier missiles are powered by a solid-fuel rocket motor, and have a range of 450–7,500yd (400–6,800m), with a 1.4kg fragmentation explosive close-proximity warhead triggered by a chemical fuse. Two missiles are mounted on either side of the unit.

Until the Marconi Blindfire radar system was introduced into British Army service in 1979, a Rapier battery consisted of a pair of Land Rover forward-control '101' gun tractors, one towing the missile launcher, the other carrying stores, with a third vehicle towing the Blindfire unit.

By 1989 the '101' had been replaced by the special winch-equipped Marshall-bodied Defender 127 (described as the Defender 130 from 1990) gun tractor, 214 examples of which

**TOP** The Marshall-bodied Defender 127/130 gun tractor replaced the '101 FC' as the towing vehicle for the Rapier surface-to-air wire-guided missile. Similar vehicles were also built in Turkey by Otokar.

(Simon Thomson)

**ABOVE** Crew-cabbed Defender 127/130 also seen coupled to the Rapier missile battery.

(Warehouse Collection)

were delivered between October 1989 and March 1990. Designated as the 'fire unit truck' (FUT), the extended wheelbase of the Defender 127 allowed the vehicle to carry a special high-capacity pickup body with a high canvas cover. A similar vehicle was also constructed in Turkey by Otokar, for the Turkish Air Force.

Rapier is expected to remain in service until at least 2020, but the Defender 127 tractor had been phased out in favour of the Leyland-DAF 4-tonne truck by the mid-1990s.

## Wolf Defender XD

By the end of the 1980s the British Army's Land Rover fleet was looking increasingly out-dated. There were still a handful of petrol-engined Series IIIs, together with large numbers of diesel Series IIIs and Defenders, Series IIA and III 'lightweights' and the forward-control '101' gun tractors.

The Ministry of Defence (MoD) started

looking into the possibility of replacing the fleet with a new vehicle that would offer enhanced performance and increased reliability. In 1988 a specification was issued for what was being described as the 'truck, utility, light, high specification' (TUL-HS), and 'truck, utility, medium, high specification' (TUM-HS); a separate specification described the 'truck, utility, heavy' (TUH) that was intended to replace the forward-control '101', as well as providing a suitable long-wheelbase chassis for a new battlefield ambulance. The specification called for considerable improvements in overall performance when compared with the Defender, and the following was prescribed as the minimum acceptable performance:

■ Towing capability: 7,700lb (3,500kg) using over-run brakes on the trailer; 8,800lb (4,000kg) with power brakes.
■ Maximum under-vehicle angle: 155°.
■ Mean maximum ground pressure: 51lbf/in$^2$ (350kPa).
■ Minimum approach and departure angles: front 40°, rear 38°.
■ Minimum turning circle: 40ft (12m).
■ Static stability on side-slope: maximum 33°.
■ Unprepared fording depth: 24in (600mm).

The MoD contacted 19 manufacturers to gauge interest in the project and an invitation to tender was issued in November 1991. Just three companies indicated that they were prepared to

submit detailed bids: Land Rover, IVECO-Ford and Automotive Technik Pinzgauer, the latter two being eliminated from the process without even being asked to submit vehicles. A contract was issued to Land Rover for the construction of 'evaluation trials' vehicles.

Land Rover assigned the name Wolf to the project, and the first round of trials vehicles – which were delivered in May 1993 – were eventually described as Wolf-1. Although the vehicle was powered by the 300Tdi 2,495cc turbocharged diesel engine that was to appear in the civilian line-up for 1994, Wolf-1 was little more than an improved 'core military' Defender. There was a side-mounted tailgate carrying the spare wheel, and the long-wheelbase TUM-HS chassis was fitted with a front-mounted winch. Both of the 'fitted for radio' variants had a bulge on the engine cover to accommodate a 24V alternator.

Trials were conducted at the Defence Evaluation & Research Agency (DERA), where weaknesses were exposed in the transmission, axle casings and halfshafts, differentials, steering gear and suspension, whilst both the chassis and body were found to be lacking structural integrity. The trials were stopped in September 1993 and DERA suggested that Land Rover prepare new prototypes for a second round of trials, giving them 12 months to develop and submit a redesigned vehicle.

Wolf-2 prototypes were submitted for trials in September 1994, showing significant improvements in virtually all areas. Both on-

**ABOVE** Wolf-1 prototype for the TUM ('truck, utility, medium') FFR role. Note the prominent bulge in the engine compartment cover that was required to provide clearance for a large alternator. *(Crown Copyright)*

**LEFT** Rear view of the Wolf-1 TUL ('truck, utility, light') variant showing the side-hung tailgate and the rear-mounted spare wheel. *(Crown Copyright)*

**LEFT** Rover also produced a Wolf-1 prototype for the TUH ('truck, utility, heavy') role, designed to replace the forward-control '101' gun tractors and ambulances. The ambulance contract was eventually won by Rover, but the gun tractor contract went to Auto Technik Pinzgauer. *(Crown Copyright)*

and off-road performance was enhanced, the payload capability was increased and there were improvements in driver safety. The 300Tdi turbocharged diesel unit was retained, with a power output of 111bhp from 2,495cc, and was coupled to the standard Land Rover five-speed gearbox and two-speed transfer case, the latter incorporating a third differential. The chassis cross-members were strengthened, and the front bulkhead, cab top rails and sills reinforced; at the rear the load bed was also strengthened and reinforced, to provide a 20 per cent payload increase. A Rover axle was used at the front, with a Salisbury unit at the rear, and in both cases the differential housings were increased in thickness to 6mm, and the halfshafts and differentials uprated compared to the 'core military' Defender. The axles were suspended on long-travel coil springs with uprated telescopic shock absorbers, and axle location was achieved by a Panhard rod and radius arm. Recirculating-ball power steering was fitted as standard, with enhanced protection for the normally exposed elements of the steering gear, and the brakes were dual servo-assisted discs. Special heavy-duty 16in perforated wheels were fitted, shod with 7.50-16 Goodyear G90 or Michelin XZL tyres. Regardless of role, the electrical system was wired for 24V using a high-output alternator, albeit the FFR power bulge of the Wolf-1 had gone. The spare wheel was moved to a side mount for safety reasons.

The smaller, 90in wheelbase TUL-HS

provided accommodation for two men in the front and four in the rear, whilst the rear body of the 110in TUM had space for eight men. Both hardtop and soft-top variants were produced, with the hardtop itself fabricated from a self-coloured polymer-composite and incorporating a vision hatch in the cab roof. For the first time in a military Land Rover, a full roll cage was fitted, together with front seat belts and anchorage points for rear belts. Around half the fleet were to be fitted for radio, the others being described as 'GS' (general service). The Wolf could also be equipped with the so-called 'weapons mount installation kit' (WMIK) that allows the vehicle to carry two 7.62mm general purpose machine guns (GPMG) or a GPMG and a .50in Browning (see page 84).

A second trials period followed, covering 55,000 miles (89,000km) over eight months. The redesigned Wolf was judged to be considerably more successful, easily meeting the stated reliability requirement. The short-wheelbase TUL-HS achieved a final 'mean distance between failure' (MDBF) figure of 11,679 miles (18,919km), whilst the TUM-HS clocked up 4,250 miles (6,885km), measured against a requirement of 2,325 miles (3,766km) on a typical simulated battlefield mission.

Wolf was unveiled to the public at the Royal Navy and British Army Equipment Exhibition (RN/BAEE) in 1995, with the production contract being awarded to Rover in February 1996. Production started later that year, and the total number of vehicles produced for the British Army was 7,925, at a reputed price of £50,000 each. Of these, 1,411 were of the short-wheelbase configuration (TUL-HS), whilst the remainder (6,514) were the long-wheelbase pattern (TUM-HS). There have been no repeat orders in Britain, but as well as serving with the British Army, Wolf is also in service with the Croatian Army, who have 30 vehicles, and the Dutch Marines, with 71 vehicles, 40 being fitted with hardtops and equipped for radio, the remainder fitted with non-standard soft tops designed to accept a Kevlar inner liner, and intended for reconnaissance and patrol duties. The Dutch Wolfs are designated XD 110 HS/WW, indicating that the vehicles are both waterproofed and winterised, and the total price for the contract (2001) was €4,324,545, giving a unit cost of €60,909.

**BELOW** Production Wolf-2 TUM vehicle – generally just described as 'Wolf' – equipped for the communications role. Note the side-mounted spare wheel, distinctive perforated steel wheels and the triangular air intake on the side of the body.
*(Phil Royal)*

Since 1996 British Army Wolfs have seen service in Iraq and in Afghanistan, where the vehicle has proved itself to be fast, reliable and extremely capable, tackling the most extreme terrain without difficulty. Some examples in service with the Royal Marines are equipped for deep-water wading, allowing them to operate fully submerged if necessary, and to undertake amphibious landing operations. A midlife rebuild may well see the bulk of the British Army Wolf fleet survive in service until 2017.

Wolf was never made available on the civilian market and even military-surplus vehicles remain scarce, most being rebuilt accident-damaged vehicles. In 1998 a fleet of arctic-prepared long-wheelbase Wolf-specification Defender 110 vehicles was constructed for a proposed Land Rover TransGlobal expedition, but the expedition was cancelled only days before the planned departure date and the vehicles were sold on the civilian market. A similar situation arose in 2003, when the German government placed an order for a fleet of Wolf high-capacity pickup trucks, vans and station wagons for use by the national security and law enforcement agencies. These vehicles were powered by either the standard 2,493cc Td5 turbocharged diesel engine, or by a 3-litre BMW engine. The contract was cancelled in late 2004, with the Wolf being superseded by the Mercedes-Benz *Gelandewagen*, and those vehicles that had been delivered were similarly disposed of on the civilian market.

**LEFT** The British Army took delivery of 7,925 examples of the Wolf, of which 1,411 were of the short-wheelbase TUL configuration seen here. Examples were also supplied to Croatia and the Netherlands. *(Land Rover Limited)*

**ABOVE** A planned midlife rebuild should see the Wolf remaining in service with the British Army until 2017. *(Warehouse Collection)*

**BELOW** Wolf TUL 'medevac' vehicle photographed at Camp Bastion in Afghanistan. *(MoD, Corporal Steven Peacock)*

**BELOW** Wolf TUM equipped with the Ricardo weapons mount installation kit that serves as a combined roll-over protection system and weapons mount. *(MoD)*

'The versatile Defender range can mount an incredibly wide array of weapons – from machine guns to anti-tank and anti-aircraft missiles... rapid deployment and mobility will be the key to tomorrow's peacekeeping.'

**Land Rover Limited military sales leaflet**
1988

## Chapter Four

# Conversion to role

Generally described as a 'utility vehicle', the standard role of the military Land Rover is to transport cargo and personnel across 'improved and unimproved roads'. However, the sheer versatility of the vehicle, combined with its low price and ability to tackle most types of terrain, made it an ideal candidate for conversion at base or unit level to a variety of more specialised roles, including weapons mount, signals line layer, workshop and recovery vehicle. Some of these conversions are permanent, others are relatively easily reversible.

OPPOSITE **Based on the Defender 110, and constructed by Marshalls of Cambridge, the Land Rover DPV was typical of Special Forces vehicles since the appearance of the SAS Jeep in this role during World War Two.** *(Phil Royal)*

Although the Series I Land Rover was criticised by the Army for its 'flimsy' aluminium alloy bodywork, it does not seem to have deterred the War Office from adapting the vehicle to a variety of roles. Many might consider Land Rover's slogan – 'the world's most versatile vehicle' – to be no more than marketing 'puff', but as far as the vehicle's military roles are concerned it is no idle boast. The list of 'FV' numbers (see Table 2, page 153) gives some idea of the number of roles in which the vehicle was eventually used; and remember that this is not even a comprehensive list, since this numbering system had been abandoned by about 1980.

Some specialised roles require the vehicle to be practically rebuilt, others need rather less elaborate modification. Amongst the latter group are those of gun tractor, bomb disposal vehicle, liaison vehicle or command car, and royal/officer review vehicle. As regards more permanent conversion, ambulance bodies have been built and fitted by companies such as Locomotors, Mann Egerton, Marshalls of Cambridge, Mickleover Transport and Park Royal Vehicles. Marshalls of Cambridge have also frequently been called upon to convert standard vehicles to the special operations role, most famously undertaking the final development and construction of the SAS Regiment's iconic Series IIA 'Pink Panthers'. Latterly it has been Ricardo Engineering who have upgraded the Defender platform for use by Special Forces, fitting their weapons mount installation kit. Armoured vehicles have been produced by the likes of Glover & Webb, Hotspur Armoured Products, Penman Engineering, and Short Brothers &

Harland (Shorland), and military fire appliances constructed by Carmichael, Foamite and HCB-Angus.

As regards one-offs and low-volume specialised conversions, examples include vehicles that have been armoured and equipped with railway wheels to be used for track patrol work, helicopter-starting vehicles, and welding shop, recovery and workshop vehicles. Many of these conversions have been carried out in REME workshops, at unit level or even in the field.

# Ambulance

With its relatively small size and go-anywhere ability, the Land Rover lends itself well to adaptation to the role of battlefield or off-road ambulance, and this was one of the earliest specialised roles assigned to the vehicle. Indeed, Land Rover ambulances remain in service to the present day.

### Expedient field ambulance

During World War Two the Jeep had been adapted for use as an expedient field ambulance by the British, American and Australian Armies using a variety of different ambulance conversion systems, including the Janes, the Edwards, the Australian airborne and the Carter. The last produced a simple field ambulance from a standard ¼-ton utility vehicle – either the Jeep, Champ or Land Rover Series I – without compromising its basic role.

In late 1957 the FVRDE tested the Carter ambulance conversion on an 86in Series I, to see if the same equipment could be standardised between the Champ and the Land Rover. The stretcher gear consisted of two pairs of channel-section rails carried on brackets attached to the rear body, and supported on a tubular cross-member just behind the front seats. The stretchers were simply slid into position along the rails and secured by webbing straps, protruding more than two feet behind the vehicle. There was a snout-like canvas extension to the rear of the canopy to provide a degree of weather protection to the patients.

Two trial installations were made, with the first employing the brackets and fittings designed for use with the Champ and requiring

**BELOW Series I adapted for the Carter ambulance conversion. A pair of stretchers were carried in rails fitted to the rear body, but the length of the vehicle meant that the lower half of the patient was actually outside the vehicle, protected only by the snout-like canvas canopy extension.**
*(Tank Museum)*

considerable modification to the Land Rover body. The second required new mounting and support brackets to be developed and avoided body modifications, but was considered the more practical, with installation described as a 'unit modification' requiring about 16 man-hours' work. It is unlikely that these devices were ever used in anger. Indeed, the report of the trial concluded with the words 'as a compromise method for evacuating stretcher cases from a forward area under rough conditions of travel, the ride provided for a casualty by this installation is just tolerable'.

## RAF crash-rescue ambulance

The RAF mountain crash-rescue service was established in 1942 by Flight-Lieutenant F.W. Graham, and was originally based at RAF Llandwrog using Jeeps and Humber ambulances. The service picked up its first survivor in July 1943, and more than 30 aircrew had been located and evacuated by the time the team had completed its first year of operation. The following year responsibility for the work was passed to the Air Ministry and the original team was relocated to Valley on the Isle of Anglesey; three more teams were established at other stations, and by 1950 nine teams were at work. By the middle of the decade it was obvious that the Jeeps were getting rather too long in the tooth and the RAF drew up a specification for a mountain rescue vehicle using a Land Rover Series I with a purpose-built ambulance body. With its off-road capability, it was hoped that the Land Rover could fulfil the search and rescue roles of both the Jeep and the Humber.

The chassis initially chosen for the role was the standard 107in (Rover 4) pickup truck and station wagon. A full-width enclosed body, with a domed roof and a 'Luton' box over the cab, was mated to the standard Land Rover cab and front end. The rear body had an overall length of 190in (4,826mm), giving a huge rear overhang, and the vehicle has always looked to be somewhat over-bodied, but the size of the body provided sufficient space for either six seated cases, two stretcher cases and an attendant or three seated patients together with a stretcher case and an attendant. The body was framed and panelled in aluminium, with thermal insulation material fitted into the cavity between

the inner and outer skins. Small, shuttered windows were installed high in the body sides towards the rear, and there were also windows in the rear doors; external lockers were fitted on either side ahead of the rear wheel arches. There was no direct access between the cab and the body, but there were side-hinged double doors at the rear. For the comfort of patients and crew, a hot-water interior heating system was installed, with a fresh air intake at the front and twin blowers to distribute heat around the interior. Despite the additional demands made on the electrical system, the standard 12V configuration was retained.

The first batch of 11 vehicles, designated FV18005, was constructed by commercial-vehicle body builders Bonallack & Sons, of Basildon, Essex; a second batch of 14 vehicles followed in 1957, but further batches of

**LEFT** The long-wheelbase chassis of the Series I was used as the basis of a mountain rescue ambulance by the RAF. A similar body was subsequently mounted on the Series II/IIA and Series III chassis. *(Warehouse Collection)*

**BELOW** Following the lead of the RAF, the British Army also employed the long-wheelbase Series I (and later) chassis to mount a fully-enclosed two/four-stretcher ambulance body built by Marshalls of Cambridge, Mickleover Transport and Park Royal Vehicles. *(IWM, MVE31366-1)*

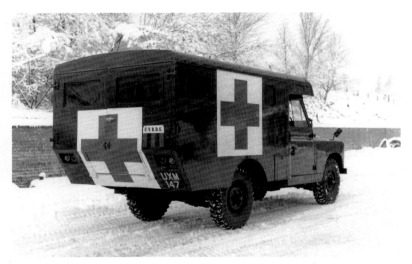

mountain rescue ambulances were constructed on the 109in wheelbase Series II (Rover 7) and Series III chassis, designated FV18043, FV18055, FV18066, FV18068 and FV18074.

### Army Series II, IIA and III ambulance

In 1962 the Army took delivery of the first of a batch of two-stretcher front-line ambulances, designated FV18008. Similar in appearance to the RAF mountain rescue vehicles, the bodies were constructed by Marshalls of Cambridge, Mickleover Transport and Park Royal Vehicles.

The body was reduced in overall height to

allow the vehicles to be carried in a transport aircraft, and there was a second side window, positioned towards the front end. The long rear overhang remained, but on most examples the body was cut away at an angle behind the rear wheel to improve the departure angle. Large-section 7.50-16 tyres were fitted, the front and rear axles were reinforced, and the standard suspension modified to improve the ride comfort. Inside there was a pair of rails designed to accept collapsible stretchers at a high level, and racks were also fitted along the roof to stow a second pair of collapsible stretchers.

When the Series I was superseded by the Series II (Rover 7), the design of the body remained virtually unchanged, although it was now described as a two/four-stretcher ambulance, and the vehicles were designated FV18044 and FV18054. The Series II was superseded by the Series IIA (Rover 9, Rover 11) in 1964–65, and the designation became FV18065 and FV18067. In 1971 the Series III replaced the Series IIA, and the ambulance designation became FV18065, FV18067 and FV18073. More than 2,000 of these vehicles were eventually acquired, with most being passed to the Territorials when the '101' forward-control ambulances started to enter service during the 1980s.

Similar vehicles were used by the Royal

ABOVE Series III-based ambulance with the large brush guard typical of many RAF vehicles. *(Phil Royal)*

RIGHT Australian Defence Force Series II ambulance showing the cut-away mudguards and lack of sills typical of ADF vehicles. *(Mike Cecil)*

Netherlands Army, based on diesel-engined Series III chassis, and the Australian Defence Force. The Spanish Santana 109 *Militar* chassis was also used as the basis of an ambulance with a locally-built body.

## Forward-control '101' ambulance

The forward-control '101' chassis was bodied by Marshalls of Cambridge as a battlefield ambulance, and for the first time the body – which was capable of accommodating two or four stretcher cases, one or two stretcher cases plus four seated patients, or eight seated patients – was integral with the cab. There were twin doors at the rear, and interior ventilation

RIGHT The Marshall-bodied 'FC 101' ambulances were still in service with the British Army during the liberation of Kuwait in 1991, and continued to serve to the end of the decade. *(Phil Royal)*

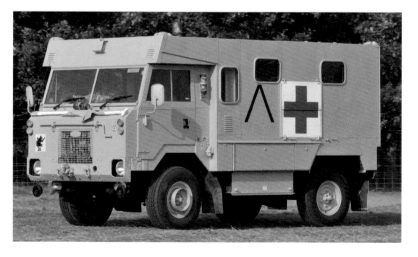

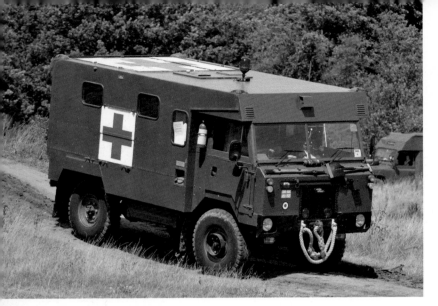

## Defender 110 and 127/130 ambulances

The Defender 110 and 127 vehicles, the latter subsequently renamed 130, were introduced for military service in the mid-1980s, and both chassis lent themselves well to the ambulance role, with the 127/130 being more generally favoured because of its additional length. As part of the 'core military' Defender range, Land Rover offered a battlefield ambulance constructed on either chassis with a body provided by either Locomotors or Marshalls of Cambridge. The sales literature stated that the body could be constructed for carrying up to six stretcher cases, or eight seated casualties, while heating or air conditioning equipment could be provided as required. Some early examples were not provided with the distinctive 'Luton' cab roof, but the ambulance body generally followed the already-established principles, albeit now with a linking door that allowed entry to the rear compartment from the cab. Windows were provided on the right-hand side, and a large stowage rack was frequently fitted on the roof. The body was updated in 1989, when the roof was squared off and the flat header panel above the windscreen replaced by a panel of a more angular shape.

**ABOVE The 'FC 101' carries Red Cross marking on the sides, roof and rear; those on the side are split and hinged across the centre and can be easily concealed if required. The boxy body is capable of accommodating two or four stretcher cases, one or two stretcher cases plus four seated, or eight seated patients.** *(Phil Royal)*

and heating facilities were provided, as well as an oxygen supply. The electrical system incorporated a high-output 24V alternator, with a split charging system. Those vehicles intended for the RAF crash-rescue role also included engine pre-heating facilities, a trickle charger and radio installation; and there were also stowage facilities for oxygen/nitrous oxide gas cylinders.

A total of 520 vehicles was constructed, all of them converted from the basic cargo vehicle, the right-hand-drive version designated FV19009 and the left-hand-drive FV19010. A total of 127 went to the RAF, the remainder serving with the Army, and the vehicles remained in service until the late 1990s, seeing action in the Balkans, Cyprus and the Middle East. They were eventually replaced by the Defender XD-130 Pulse ambulance. Around 57 '101' ambulances were also used by the Luxembourg Army.

**BELOW LEFT The old Series II/IIA and Series III ambulances were replaced by the Defender 127/130 ambulance in about 1989. In British service the ambulance was generally powered by the 3.5-litre V8 petrol engine, and the six-stretcher body was constructed by either Locomotors or Marshalls of Cambridge.** *(Ian Young)*

**BELOW A pair of Defender 127/130 airfield crash-rescue ambulances, in which the body lacks the more usual side windows.** *(Ian Young)*

There was plenty of stowage space for medical equipment, and mobile clinics, vaccination units and other medical facilities could also be supplied in the same body.

Small numbers of Defender 127/130 ambulances were purchased by all three of the British services, generally powered by the 3.5-litre V8 petrol engine, but from 1996 they were effectively superseded by the Defender XD-130 Pulse.

However, for export customers the Defender 130 continues to be offered for this role, with Land Rover equally happy to supply customers with chassis-cab vehicles for local body construction. For example, the Irish Defence Force has procured a small number of Defender 130s fitted with two-stretcher ambulance bodies constructed by Macclesfield Motor Bodies of Cheshire, whilst the Royal Netherlands Army asked Marshalls of Cambridge to construct a box body for the same chassis. Military ambulance bodies for the Defender 130 have also been constructed by Macclesfield Motor Bodies, Pilcher-Greene, Singapore Technologies Kinetics and the Shanning Group, the last taking the form of a removable pod that can be fitted into the back of a standard long-wheelbase cargo vehicle.

## XD-130 Pulse ambulance

Alongside the 90in and 110in Wolf XD Defender TUL and TUM variants, the Ministry of Defence also specified a third version of the XD chassis with a nominal 130in wheelbase – although, as with the Defender 130, it actually measured

127in. Described as the TUH ('truck, utility, heavy'), the truck was designed to replace the forward-control '101' gun tractors and ambulances, as well as a motley collection of existing military ambulances, including the ageing, and increasingly unreliable Marshall-bodied Series IIA and Series III vehicles (which could trace their origins back to 1956) and the coil-sprung Defender 127/130.

A box-bodied 127/130in ambulance had always been envisaged as one of the standard variants of the Wolf XD range, and the initial General Statement of Requirements (GSR) that described the vehicle had been prepared in 1991. Invitations to bid were issued to three companies in June 1992, and it was envisaged that trials for the vehicle would run alongside the later stages of those for the standard Wolf utility vehicles. As before, the contenders for the role included IVECO-Ford, with a development

**ABOVE Removable ambulance 'pod' installed in the rear of a Defender 110 pickup.** *(Roland Groom, Tank Museum)*

**LEFT Australian Defence Force Perentie 6x6 ambulance being loaded on to a Landing Craft, Medium 8 (LCM8) from Herald Island, during Exercise Squadex 2012, the first of two exercises in which Australia's newest ship, HMAS *Choules*, conducted amphibious and flying operations with elements of the Australian Army.** *(Australian Department of Defence)*

of the 40.10WM, and Automotive Technik with the Pinzgauer 710.

The Land Rover ambulance – dubbed 'XD-130 Pulse' – was unveiled at the Royal Navy, British Army Equipment Exhibition in September 1995. However, during the trials phase of the project the Pinzgauer performed so well that it resulted in changes to the MoD's test methods, forcing the designers at Land Rover and body-builders Marshalls of Cambridge to reconsider aspects of their design. It was only at the conclusion of the trials that the gap between the two vehicles had narrowed sufficiently to keep Wolf in the running, but in terms of 'battlefield mission' performance and 'noise, vibration, harshness' the Pinzgauer emerged as the clear winner.

Struggling to secure the contract, Land Rover emphasised user familiarity and the

commonality of components with other vehicles in the fleet, and offered a five-year vehicle warranty. It did the trick, and six months later the MoD announced that it intended to award the contract for the supply of 800 ambulances to Land Rover, 'subject to the satisfactory conclusion of contract negotiations'. A separate contract, worth £15 million, was awarded to Marshalls of Cambridge, whilst Pinzgauer secured the gun tractor contract. The first Pulse ambulances entered service in late 1996, and the vehicle has now replaced all Series IIA and Series III leaf-sprung ambulances, as well as most of the 127/130 ambulances in British Army service. Essentially the same body has also been adapted for the command and communications role.

Despite sharing the basic cab and most of its automotive equipment with the TUL/ TUM variants, Pulse has the unmistakeable 'over-bodied' appearance of the typical British Army ambulance, with increased width at the rear, and a large overhang behind the rear wheels. The two-man cab is connected via a door to a large, box-shaped walk-through rear body equipped to carry four standard NATO stretchers, with semi-automatic loading equipment to reduce the need for manual lifting. The stretcher arrangements allow the vehicle to also carry two stretcher and three seated casualties, or six seated patients. There is air conditioning and heating equipment, with a separate fuel-burning heater in the rear body, together with stowage facilities for the crew's personal equipment, oxygen bottles, resuscitation equipment, etc.

The MoD has recently suggested that up to 300 Pulse ambulances could be surplus to requirements from the year 2015, and has demonstrated how they might be converted to a convoy escort vehicle or mortar carrier. A demonstration vehicle, dubbed 'Project Hebe', was shown at the Defence Vehicle Dynamics Show (DVD) in 2010, fitted with a hardtop four-man crew cab and a tail-gated pickup body with a capacity of 1,750–2,200lb (800–1,000kg).

## Anti-tank

The expression 'shoot-and-scoot' is often used to describe the actions of a small, highly manoeuvrable vehicle with anti-tank capability. The earliest vehicles of this type appeared during World War Two, taking the form of Jeeps equipped with American recoilless rifles (RCLR). Inevitably the Land Rover was also seen as a suitable candidate for this role, and, as well as the American M40 106mm recoilless rifle and the later British weapons of this type – including the WOMBAT ('weapon of magnesium, battalion anti-tank') and MOBAT ('mobile battalion anti-tank') – has also commonly been used as a mount for a range of wire-guided anti-tank missiles.

### M40 106mm recoilless rifle

By the mid-1950s the original American 75mm recoilless rifle had been superseded by the 106mm M40 weapon firing high-explosive anti-tank (HEAT), high-explosive squash-head (HESH), high-explosive plastic tracer (HEP-T) and anti-personnel rounds (APERS-T). A co-axial M8C spotting rifle was mounted above the barrel, allowing the gunner to check his aim and trajectory before firing an expensive anti-tank round; in later guns, a laser sighting device was used for the same purpose. The weapon was able to penetrate 150mm of armour at a 60° impact angle, with an effective range of 1,200yd (1,098m), and was extensively deployed during the Korean War and in Vietnam, as well as being in widespread service across the world.

In the British Army the M40 was mounted on 88in Series I and II/IIA Land Rovers until the late 1950s, when it started to be replaced by the MOBAT and WOMBAT guns. Elsewhere the M40

remained a popular low-cost anti-tank weapon and could be found mounted on a variety of vehicles, including the Defender 90 and 110 and the Spanish Santana Model 88 *Militar*.

In November 1976 Marshalls of Cambridge showed an M40A1 recoilless rifle, supplied by the Pakistan Machine Tool Factory, mounted on the 'lightweight' Land Rover as part of an order for around 100 vehicles for the Saudi-Arabian National Guard. The rifle was carried on the standard M79 tripod mount, giving a 180° arc of fire forwards and remaining easily dismountable for firing in a ground position. The standard vehicle windscreen was replaced by a rubber-glazed split screen that allowed the gun barrel to be traversed over the bonnet and clamped in the travelling position. Side-facing drop-down seats were fitted in the rear,

and there was an additional under-seat fuel tank to compensate for the increased fuel consumption, as well as ammunition stowage lockers/bins. Blast shields were fitted to protect the mudguards, engine cover and spare wheel when firing forwards. The vehicles entered service in 1977, with some seeing action during the liberation of Kuwait.

The Dutch Marines also used 88in 'lightweights' in this role, but without body modifications, and the Spanish Army mounted licence-built Cetme 105mm recoilless rifles on the 88in Series I.

### Carl Gustav

Designed by the Swedish Bofors company (now SAAB Bofors Dynamics), the 84mm Carl Gustav recoilless rifle appeared in 1946, entering service with the Swedish Army two years later. It quickly became one of the standard NATO infantry anti-tank weapons, was eventually deployed by more than 40 nations across the world – including Britain and the United States – and despite its age remains in widespread use today. An improved M2 variant was introduced in 1964, with the current lightweight M3 version dating from 1991. The maximum range for a stationary target is 765yd (700m), reducing to around 437yd (400m) if the target is moving.

The US Army 75th Ranger Regiment has deployed the Carl Gustav weapon – in the form of the Rangers' anti-tank weapon system (RAWS) – on its Land Rover special operations vehicle (SOV). Land Rover also include the Carl Gustav in a list of standard weapons that can be mounted on the Defender chassis.

**BELOW** The US Rangers' SOV normally carried the Carl Gustav 84mm recoilless rifle, which was described as the Rangers' anti-tank weapon system. In this photograph the RAWS has been placed on the ground alongside the front wheel. *(US DoD, Michael Lemke)*

## WOMBAT and MOBAT recoilless rifles

The first British 'battalion anti-tank' (BAT) recoilless rifle system appeared in the late 1940s in the form of the L1 BAT, firing 120mm high-explosive squash-head (HESH) ammunition designed to flatten out against the target, generating a stream of molten metal that causes internal spalling of the armour. Proving to be too large and unwieldy for effective deployment, BAT was replaced by the lighter L4 MOBAT ('mobile battalion anti-tank') in 1959. Developed by the Royal Armaments Research & Development Establishment (RARDE) at Fort Halstead, MOBAT was designed to fire similar 120mm squash-head rounds, with a maximum range of about 900yd (885m). The gun was designed to be towed, muzzle first, on a small two-wheeled carriage, behind a Land Rover or Champ.

In the early 1960s, MOBAT was replaced by the lightweight L6 WOMBAT ('weapon of magnesium, battalion anti-tank'). By this time the range of the L1 round had been extended to about 1,000yd (983m) against a static target, and 800yd (787m) against a moving target. Where MOBAT had used a co-axial 0.303in Bren as a spotting rifle, for WOMBAT this was replaced by the L40A1 12.7mm gun derived from the American M8C.

Lightweight alloys were widely used in its construction meaning that WOMBAT weighed just 650lb (295kg), compared to the 1,650lb (750kg) of MOBAT. The weight was also reduced by removing all unnecessary components and equipment – even the standard towed carriage was eliminated in favour of a post mount carried on a lightweight close-spaced axle assembly. WOMBAT did not include any towing provision – the wheels simply allowed the gun to be manoeuvred into a firing position, while for transport the gun was carried in a 'portee'. Early trials photographs showed the 'WOMBAT kit' installed in an 88in Series II (Rover 6) before attention turned to adapting the 109in long-wheelbase Series II (Rover 7). In the latter case the gun was carried further back, allowing sufficient space for a driver and the three-man crew, as well as stowage racks for six spare rounds behind the front seats. The gun was normally fired from a dug-in position, but in an emergency could be

**RIGHT** Short-wheelbase Series II/IIA into which has been loaded the British Army WOMBAT on its two-wheeled carriage. Although normally dismounted before use, in an emergency the weapon could be fired from the vehicle, providing the barrel was deployed at right angles to the centreline of the chassis. *(Tank Museum)*

used without dismounting it from the vehicle, providing the barrel was deployed at right angles to the centreline of the chassis.

In this form WOMBAT entered British Army service in 1962, described as 'recoilless anti-tank gun truck mount' (FV18045), on a Series IIA chassis (Rover 9). The weapon was used in the Falklands in 1981, although by that time it was already considered to be obsolete, replacement by the MILAN anti-tank missile having begun in the late 1970s (see page 68).

## Vickers Vigilant missile

Introduced in 1956, the Vickers Vigilant was a lightweight wire-guided anti-tank missile with a 12lb (5.5kg) shaped hollow-charge warhead and an effective range of 1,500yd (1,372m). As well as being man-portable, Vigilants were also helicopter- and vehicle-mounted, notably using the long-wheelbase Series II and IIA (Rover 6, Rover 9). In one early scheme the missiles were launched from a tripod in the rear of the Land Rover, whilst a later variant carried a dozen, designed to be dismounted and ground launched as required. Trials were also conducted in which four and six Vigilants were carried in a modular launch frame that allowed the missiles to be fired in pairs without requiring them to be dismounted from the back of the vehicle.

## BAC Swingfire missile

In 1960 the British Aircraft Corporation (BAC) introduced Swingfire, a reliable and accurate wire-guided anti-tank missile carrying a 15lb (7kg) hollow charge, with an effective range

**RIGHT** Mounting WOMBAT in the long-wheelbase Land Rover allowed the windscreen to remain in place, but nevertheless this was a sizeable piece of kit and there was a considerable rear overhang. *(Warehouse Collection)*

of 166–4,375yd (150–4,000m) on stationary or moving targets. Swingfire was said to be capable of penetrating up to 32in (800mm) of armour, making it more than a match for even the heaviest tanks of the Warsaw Pact. The ability to separate the launch mechanism and

**BELOW** Close-up view of the business end of WOMBAT, this time in a long-wheelbase Series II/IIA. *(Warehouse Collection)*

**LEFT** The British Aircraft Corporation Swingfire was a wire-guided anti-tank missile system said to be capable of penetrating up to 32in (800mm) of armour. In 1969 BAC demonstrated a multi-missile Swingfire system, dubbed Beeswing, mounted onto one of the early prototypes for what became the forward-control '101'. *(Tank Museum)*

In 1969 BAC demonstrated a palletised version of Swingfire that could be launched from the back of a long-wheelbase Land Rover. This was followed by a multi-missile Swingfire system dubbed Beeswing that provided infantry units with a formidable tank-killing capability, and was shown mounted on one of the early prototypes for what became the forward-control '101'. Contemporary publicity material suggested that the equipment had been constructed especially for the British Army. Beeswing provided six Swingfire missiles in pairs; the flanking missiles were orientated at 45° from the centre unit to give an effective 190° coverage without requiring a launch traverser. Once the target was acquired, missiles could be fired at two-second intervals. A pair of reload missiles could also be carried in the centre launcher position, giving a total of eight missiles. The system could be broken down into convenient packages to allow it to be transported by a three-man team.

Although the British Army lost interest in this project in about 1974, BAC persevered with the idea of a vehicle-mounted Swingfire battery and in 1979 demonstrated a launcher carrying ten Swingfire missiles – four in hydraulically-operated launch tubes, and six reload missiles – mounted in a production forward-control '101'. This version may subsequently have been manufactured in Egypt under licence.

## Euromissile MILAN

Towards the end of the 1970s British infantry units had abandoned WOMBAT and Swingfire in favour of the smaller and simpler

**ABOVE** Pallet-mounted Beeswing launcher in the rear of a long-wheelbase Series II/IIA dating from the mid-1950s. The single missile is captured at the moment of launch. *(Warehouse Collection)*

sighting equipment, combined with the use of a so-called 'gathering programme', also meant that it was not necessary for the operator to fire the missile directly at the target. The launch position could remain hidden providing the target could be seen in the sights, and the 'gathering programme' brought the missile into the operator's field of view after launch, allowing it to be guided onto the target under joystick control.

**LEFT** Swingfire incorporated a separation sight that allowed the operator to fire the missiles from a dug-in position away from the vehicle. *(Tank Museum)*

MILAN ('*missile d'infanterie léger anti-char*') developed by the Franco-German Euromissile consortium, formed by Messerschmitt-Bölkow-Blohm and Aerospatiale Matra in 1972. Design work for the missile had started in the 1960s, with prototypes appearing in 1969. Production did not start in earnest until 1973, when British Aerospace joined the consortium to produce MILANs for the British Army.

MILAN is a second-generation tube-launched, spin-stabilised anti-tank guided weapon (ATGW) that provides an effective anti-tank capability for infantry units. The missile consists of a sealed high-explosive anti-tank (HEAT) warhead with a range of around 2,200yd (2,000m), which is guided to the target by a 'semi-automatic command to line of sight' (SACLOS) system operating via feedback from an infrared (IR) tracking module. Light in weight and easily adaptable, it can be launched either from the ground or from a vehicle, with the Defender 90 or 110 providing a typical vehicle mount. The system has also been mounted on the Defender 130 pickup and the Defender MRCV chassis. Other nations have used similar machines, the Belgians, for example, fitting the system to the Minerva licence-built Land Rover.

In 1984 the original missile was superseded by the improved MILAN 2, to deal with the threat of the Soviet T-72 tank, and the tandem-warhead MILAN 2T variant was announced in 1993, designed to defeat explosive reactive armour (ERA). MILAN 3 was developed to reduce susceptibility to jamming systems, and entered service in 1995.

## Other anti-tank missiles

Other anti-tank missiles deployed from the Land Rover include the Euromissile HOT ('*haut subsonique optiquement téléguidé*'), the French ENTAC system ('*engin téléguidé anti-char*') that has been used by the Australian Defence Force (ADF), the American TOW ('tube-launched, optically-tracked, wire command-link guided) system as used by the Royal Netherlands Army, and the Nimrod long-range surface-to-surface missile system developed by Israel Aerospace Industries and used by the Israeli Defence Force (IDF).

**ABOVE** Towards the end of the 1970s the British Army abandoned WOMBAT and Swingfire in favour of the smaller and simpler MILAN (*'missile d'infanterie léger anti-char'*) developed by the Euromissile consortium formed by Messerschmitt-Bölkow-Blohm and Aerospatiale Matra. Light in weight and easily adaptable, MILAN can be launched either from the ground or from a vehicle. *(Tank Museum, Roland Groom)*

**BELOW** The Belgian Army adapted 13 elderly Minerva licence-built Land Rovers to mount the MILAN anti-tank missile, with four reload missiles carried in tubes in a rack at the rear of the vehicle. *(Simon Thomson)*

## *Appliqué* armour

**ABOVE** 80in Series I Land Rover equipped with *appliqué* sheet-steel armour and steel wheels to permit deployment as a railway patrol vehicle. It is armed with a Bren gun on a simple cradle mount. *(Tank Museum)*

**BELOW** Mine-protected Series III dating from 1979, fitted with a Rhodesian Army roll-over hoop designed to make it easy to right the vehicle should it be overturned by a mine blast. Heavy steel plate has also been welded under the chassis. *(Phil Royal)*

Land Rover Series III vehicles and 'lightweights' used for patrolling in Northern Ireland were frequently protected by means of a retro-fitted vehicle protection kit (VPK). This consisted of a hardtop, *appliqué* composite GRP (glass-fibre reinforced plastic) and Makrolon ballistic-protection panels for the doors, sills and engine cover, an armoured shield for the windscreen and wire-mesh screens over the windows and lights. Twin doors were fitted at the rear and a two-man hatch was installed in the roof.

From 1992 the original VPK-equipped Land Rovers were replaced by the 'truck utility, medium (TUM) with a different vehicle protection kit (VPK)' – better known by its nickname 'Snatch'. Intended for patrolling low-threat areas, the Snatch vehicles incorporated CAMAC CAV 100 composite glass-fibre armour produced by NP Aerospace (formerly Courtaulds Aerospace), and were resistant to small arms fire and some types of improvised explosive devices (IED).

Six 'Snatch' versions have been produced. Originally there were 994 examples of Snatch-1, with 278 subsequently being 'desertised' for use in Iraq and reclassified as Snatch-1.5. Many of these were upgraded to Snatch-2 configuration: the basic Snatch-2 was a left-hand-drive vehicle with a 12V electrical system, and was generally used for training; Snatch-2A was of right-hand-drive configuration, with a 24V electrical system, and was fitted with air-conditioning equipment; whilst the 24V right-hand-drive Snatch-2B was intended for Northern Ireland. Most were originally fitted with the 3.5-litre petrol engine but were subsequently retro-fitted with the 2.5-litre 300Tdi diesel engine. A number of Snatch-2 vehicles have been further upgraded to Snatch Vixen configuration, with chassis and drive-train enhancements to increase the payload. The composite armour is supposed to be resistant to penetration by rifle fire, but it is said that insurgents in Afghanistan have weapons that 'go right through the composite'. The vehicles are also frequently fitted with electronic countermeasures equipment designed to inhibit the detonation of certain types of IED. Despite heavy criticism of the levels of protection provided – and some 37 fatalities amongst troops, who often referred to the Snatch as a 'mobile coffin' – British troops in Afghanistan were equipped with Snatch Land Rovers until about 2009.

**ABOVE** Prototype Snatch vehicle intended for patrolling low-threat areas. Protected by CAMAC CAV 100 composite glass-fibre armour produced by NP Aerospace, Snatch vehicles were resistant to small arms fire and some types of improvised explosive devices. *(Tank Museum)*

**ABOVE** Originally designed for use in Northern Ireland, the composite armoured Snatch proved completely unsuitable for service in Iraq and Afghanistan. Dubbed 'mobile coffins' by those obliged to use them for patrols, the vehicles contributed to some 37 deaths due to roadside bombs. *(MoD)*

**LEFT** The final version of Snatch was described as the Snatch Vixen, and was effectively a Snatch-2 vehicle that had been further upgraded with chassis and drivetrain enhancements to increase the payload. *(MoD, Corporal Russ Nolan)*

Other armoured Land Rovers used in Northern Ireland by the Royal Ulster Constabulary (RUC) and, latterly, by the Police Service of Northern Ireland (PSNI) include the Tangi, either with a 3.5-litre petrol engine or the Td5 diesel, plus the Hotspur, Shenzi, Simba, Tenba and Pangolin, the last constructed by the OVIK Group and procured in 2011. Most of the work on these vehicles was carried out in the workshops of the RUC/PSNI under the watchful eye of Ernie Lusty, creator of the original Shorland armoured car (see page 90), with constant improvement in response to experience gained on the streets. Tangi, for example, was eventually produced in six different types.

**LEFT** All Snatch Land Rovers have now been withdrawn from conventional frontline service, and whilst many have been disposed of through Witham Specialist Vehicles it was reported in the summer of 2011 that around 50 were to be converted to remote-controlled 'drones' for use in Afghanistan. MIRA was awarded the £15 million development contract. *(Ian Young)*

**RIGHT** Resembling a standard Land Rover Defender 110, the Hobson Ranger has been protected to STANAG Level 1 using a combination of steel and Makrolon composite armour.
*(Warehouse Collection)*

In 2008–9 Hobson Industries announced the Ranger, an armoured vehicle based on an upgraded Defender 110 chassis, protected to STANAG Level 1 using a combination of steel and Makrolon composite armour. The company also supplies an *appliqué* steel armour kit for the Defender that provides ballistic protection. The kit can be fitted by two men and requires no welding, being simply bolted on to the vehicle structure using the tools provided.

A new demountable armour system (DAS), designed by the Labbé division of Armor Holdings Inc, has recently been made available for the Defender. The DAS is intended for use by aid agencies and others working in vulnerable areas, and consists of a kit of armoured components that can be attached to a base vehicle as required. The vehicle must be fitted with a special heavy-duty bulkhead in order to accept the armour.

## Command vehicle

Produced by Searle Limited of Sunbury, the Carawagon was a popular camping conversion of the long-wheelbase Land Rover. Towards the end of the 1970s the company produced the first of possibly 34 military command vehicles, based on the civilian Carawagon, for use in Germany. Identification features included the large roof rack fitted forward of the cab, blacked-out windows along the left-hand side, and, when erected, the high semi-circular roof that provided internal headroom. Inside was a desk or work surface, stowage facilities, cooker, fridge, and sink etc.

## Fire-fighting

In 1952 Rover constructed a small fire appliance on one of the pre-production chassis. Equipped with a self-priming Pegson pump, a 40-gallon (180-litre) 'first aid' water

tank and two delivery hoses, it was intended for use in a factory or, for example, a power station or woodland estate. Whilst the numbers constructed were never large, the Land Rover remained a popular basis for conversion into a fire appliance, and the vehicle's off-road performance made it very suitable for military fire-fighting applications, including airfield fire-crash-rescue and domestic fire-fighting duties. The Australian Defence Force (ADF) has also employed Land Rover-based fire appliances in both the domestic and fire-crash-rescue roles, in the latter case using a 'drop-in' pod-type fire-fighting body.

**ABOVE** Carawagon command vehicle conversion. When in the travelling mode, the domed roof extension is normally collapsed flat. The body includes facilities for working, cooking and washing.
*(Phil Royal)*

### Fire-crash-rescue

The first Land Rover-based vehicle for airfield fire-crash-rescue duties was constructed on the 109in Series II (Rover 7) in 1959–60, and was designated FV18047. Described as 'truck, fire fighting, airfield crash and rescue' (ACRT), it was designed to meet Air Ministry requirements for rapid intervention rescue facilities for crashed aircraft, and to deal with aircraft brake fires. The development work was undertaken by FVRDE working with the Air Ministry: FVRDE was responsible for the modifications required to the basic vehicle, whilst the Air Ministry

specified the fire-fighting equipment. The specialised equipment was supplied and installed by Feltham-based Foamite Limited and consisted of twin high-pressure foam extinguishers and a monitor gun, water, Pyrene and carbon-dioxide portable fire extinguishers, and asbestos blankets. Additional equipment included twin air bottles, rotary air-driven saws and other small rescue tools, searchlights, a fire bell, an extending site-illuminating light, and a two-section extending ladder. A radio telephone was fitted between the two seats. At the front there was a large welded brush guard to protect the radiator, and a revolving beacon was usually fitted on the offside front mudguard. There was no tailgate or rear tilt, and the spare wheel was removed from its normal position on the engine cover. The two-man cab included a twin-skinned roof panel into which was installed a hinged circular hatch to allow access to the searchlight.

When the Series II was superseded in 1961 the same equipment was installed on the Series IIA (Rover 9) chassis, with about 140 examples constructed. Within a decade or so the vehicle was replaced by the 'truck, aircraft, crash rescue' (TACR-1).

### TACR-1, TAC-T

A more modern rapid intervention fire-crash-rescue vehicle started to appear in 1970 using the Series IIA chassis, with production continuing until 1976 – by which time the Series III was being used. The vehicle was fitted with an aluminium body constructed and equipped by HCB-Angus of Totton, near Southampton, and perhaps by others, and was described as 'truck, aircraft crash, rescue, Mk 1' (TACR), later to be re-designated TACR-1 when the Range Rover-based TACR-2 was introduced.

The body included rear-facing equipment lockers protected by roller shutters. Dry-powder extinguishers and water-pumping equipment were carried inside the body, and there was also a 100-gallon (454-litre) 'first aid' water tank. A large square hatch in the cab roof allowed a crew member to tackle a fire from an elevated position at a safe distance, and there was an extending aluminium ladder carried on the right-hand side. Similar vehicles were also supplied to the Royal Navy for use at naval flying stations.

**RIGHT** Series II/IIA-based fire-crash-rescue truck (FV18047) designed for the RAF. With specialised equipment supplied and installed by Foamite Limited, the truck carried twin high-pressure foam extinguishers and a monitor gun, as well as asbestos blankets, and water, Pyrene and carbon-dioxide portable fire extinguishers. *(Warehouse Collection)*

**RIGHT** Front view of the FV18047 fire-crash-rescue truck showing the typical RAF brush guard. *(Tank Museum)*

**RIGHT** Rear view of the RAF fire-crash-rescue vehicle showing coiled hoses, fire extinguishers, oxygen bottles, etc. Designed to provide rapid intervention rescue facilities for crashed aircraft, the vehicle was also equipped to deal with aircraft brake fires. *(Tank Museum)*

**ABOVE LEFT** In 1970 FV18047 was superseded by the better-equipped 'truck, aircraft crash, rescue, Mk 1' (TACR, later known as TACR-1). Constructed by HCB-Angus, the vehicle carried dry-powder extinguishers and water-pumping equipment inside the body, and there was also a 100-gallon (454-litre) 'first-aid' water tank. *(Paul Hazell)*

**ABOVE RIGHT** Well-restored TACR-1 showing the equipment lockers at the rear and the roof-mounted ladder, blue lamp and searchlight. The compartment between the two lockers allows a third, fire-suited, crew member to be carried to the scene of a fire. *(Paul Hazell)*

**ABOVE** With large amounts of on-board equipment, plus nigh on a ton of water placed in the centre of the chassis, the TACR-1 certainly needed its heavy-duty axles and oversized tyres. *(Simon Thomson)*

**RIGHT** Constructed by Carmichael, Gloster-Saro and HCB-Angus, the TACR-2 rapid-response vehicle was based on a six-wheeled (originally 6x4) conversion of the Range Rover. *(Phil Royal)*

**ABOVE TAC-T ('truck, aircraft crash, tactical') entered service in 1971 in support of the Harrier programme. Constructed by Scottorn and Pyrene, it featured a powered trailer carrying 300 gallons (1,362 litres) of water, and was also capable of pumping foam.** *(Simon Thomson)*

In 1971 TACR-1 was joined by the 'truck, aircraft crash, tactical' (TAC-T), with a total of 14 examples constructed by Scottorn and Pyrene. Development of TAC-T had started back in 1967 but had been held back because of delays in the Harrier programme, for which the vehicle was intended. Although it was similarly based on the long-wheelbase Series IIA, TAC-T differed in appearance, and by virtue of the fact that it was designed to be accompanied by a Scottorn Bushmaster powered trailer carrying 300 gallons (1,362 litres) of water; the trailer effectively gave the vehicle a 6x6 drive-line, allowing it to operate in more difficult terrain. As with TACR-1, there were dry-powder extinguishers to deal with fires in aircraft brakes, but TAC-T was also capable of pumping foam as well as water using a Coventry-Climax pump in the rear compartment. The increased

on-board capacity also meant that it could be used to extinguish an entire aircraft fire, rather than simply acting in the rapid intervention role.

## Carmichael 'Redwing' FT/6

In about 1962 the Army Fire Service purchased some examples of the Redwing FT/6, a compact, manoeuvrable, forward-control domestic fire appliance described as being suitable for use 'at home and overseas, and for operation over narrow roads, steep gradients, and acute bends'. Pre-dating the Series II forward control, the FT/6 – one of a series of similarly-named vehicles produced by Carmichael of Worcester – was based on a standard Series II 109in chassis (Rover 9), extended at the front and converted to forward control by Carmichael & Sons, who were also the suppliers of the body and fire-fighting equipment. Confusingly, despite the forward-control conversion the War Office continued to designate the chassis as 'Rover 9'.

A Coventry-Climax centrifugal pump, driven from the gearbox power take-off, delivered water at up to 300–350 gallons per minute (1,350–1,600 litres per minute) from an on-board tank containing 140 gallons (635 litres); suction hoses were carried to allow the pump to draw from a separate water source. Delivery hoses were stowed in side lockers. An electric immersion heater in the engine cooling system reduced warm-up time, ensuring that the vehicle was ready for immediate operation, whilst an oil cooler allowed prolonged pumping with the vehicle stationary. There was room

**RIGHT The Army Fire Service purchased examples of this Redwing FT/6 forward-control domestic fire appliance. Its small size made it highly manoeuvrable, and it was described as being suitable for use 'over narrow roads, steep gradients, and acute bends'.** *(Warehouse Collection)*

in the boxy four-door body for a crew of five, together with the standard fire-fighting tools and equipment in stowage lockers. A 35ft (10.67m) extending ladder was carried on the roof.

This was not a purpose-made military vehicle and Carmichael also sought commercial sales. It is not known how many were constructed, nor how many were supplied to the Army, but a similar vehicle was also available equipped as a rapid-response appliance for dealing with aircraft fires, and at least one similar machine – equipped with foam-making equipment – was supplied to Westland Helicopters in late 1962.

### HCB-Angus Firefly

In the early 1970s a similar domestic fire-fighting vehicle was constructed for the RAF and the Army Fire Service by HCB-Angus Firefly, using the standard Series IIB 110in forward-control chassis. Designed for a crew of four, the vehicle was equipped with a 115-gallon (525-litre) 'first aid' water tank, together with hose reels and rear-mounted pumping equipment. One of these was deployed at the Royal Ordnance Factory at Featherstone, Staffordshire.

# Line-layer

O ne of the specialised roles of the Jeep during World War Two had been that of a field cable layer, providing a fast and efficient means of unreeling cable between fixed points, for example along a roadway or railway line; the same role was also allocated to the Champ. In early 1955, with the Champ having largely been passed over in favour of the cheaper Land Rover, FVRDE drew-up a specification for a cable-laying vehicle based on the Series I.

The cable-laying equipment was designed by the Signals Research & Development Establishment (SRDE) of the Royal Corps of Signals, and consisted of three separate elements. Two hoops of tubular steel were attached to the vehicle to carry ladders and poles; five reels of twisted signals cable were carried in tubular racks along the tops of the front mudguards; and cable-winding apparatus was installed on a shelf running across the cargo area, behind the rear seats. Tools and equipment were carried in racks at the rear. With the tailgate secured in the down position

and covered by a wooden duckboard to provide a foothold, the cable-layer stood at the back of the vehicle, strapped to a pair of upright poles, paying out the cable from the drum carried inside the body.

Trials showed that the additional weight placed excessive loads on the standard suspension, and the front mudguards became distorted by the weight of the cable reels. The vehicle went back to the Royal Corps of Signals in May 1956, and it was almost three years before a second vehicle was converted for the role, this time with the cable-laying equipment

**ABOVE Both the RAF and the Army Fire Service used examples of the HCB-Angus Firefly appliance, which came from the Massey-Ferguson works in Coventry but was based on the forward-control Series IIB.** *(Stuart Gibbard)*

**BELOW Series I-based line-laying vehicle designed to provide a fast and efficient means of unreeling cable between fixed points, for example along a road or railway line. Series IIs were also adapted for this role.** *(IWM, MVE34352-1)*

installed by Park Royal Vehicles Limited. The suspension was strengthened to accommodate the increased load, and the tubular hoops were connected together by longitudinal stabilisers. The cable-winding reel was now placed lower down, and although the multi-reel cable racks were still carried on the front mudguards their weight was carried by the tubular structure. There were no doors, and the spare wheel was removed from its normal position behind the front seats and carried on the engine cover. The operator stood on the closed tailgate, where he was provided with a padded frame, attached to the rear hoop of the tubular structure, to restrain his upper body. Large stowage bins were fitted to the inner rear mudguards, and a toolbox was fitted between the front bumper and the radiator.

The vehicle was subjected to roughly 1,000 miles (1,600km) of rough road and cross-country driving with no apparent ill effects on the handling, but once again it was concluded that the bodywork was not really up to this task, leading to the project being abandoned.

Six or seven more years elapsed until, in late 1963, the War Office identified an 'urgent' need for a new line-laying vehicle. The SRDE resurrected the project, this time using a short-wheelbase Series II (Rover 8), with the original equipment modified in minor ways. During October/November 1963 trials were carried out in an attempt to determine the effect of the equipment on the performance and handling of the vehicle. The resulting FVRDE report stated that the equipment mountings were 'reliable', the side overturn angles were 'satisfactory'

and the installation 'does not affect the vehicle performance and handling characteristics'. In this form the vehicle was accepted for service, and an *appliqué* kit was produced to allow existing vehicles to be modified in response to demand.

# Special Forces vehicles

Vehicles designed for use by Special Forces have their origins in the Chevrolets and Jeeps adapted for desert warfare by the Long Range Desert Group (LRDG) and the SAS (Special Air Service) during World War Two. Typically the vehicles were stripped of all unnecessary items before being stowed with fuel, water, ammunition and personal kit in every available space, allowing them to act as a self-contained base for long-range operations behind enemy lines. The Jeeps were replaced by similarly-modified Series I Land Rovers in the 1950s, and then by the iconic Series IIA 'Pink Panthers' that effectively established the basic design for the modern Special Forces vehicle.

### SAS Series I
The first post-war SAS patrol vehicle was a modified 86in Series I, officially described as 'truck, ¼ ton, 4x4, SAS, Rover Mk 3, FV18006'. The canvas top and frame, the doors, the windscreen and the centre section of the front seat were removed, and the passenger seat was modified and repositioned. A radio was installed in the rear compartment, and a large auxiliary fuel tank fitted inside the body, beneath a single rear-facing seat for the radio operator/

**BELOW LEFT AND RIGHT When the time came to replace the SAS Jeeps in the mid-1950s, the regiment chose to use the 86in and 88in Series I chassis. The doors, windscreen, top and other unnecessary equipment were removed, and stowage facilities were provided for large amounts of fuel, supplies and personal kit. This example is armed with a pair of Vickers 'K' machine guns ahead of the front-seat passenger, and an 0.30in machine gun in the rear.** *(Warehouse Collection)*

rear gunner. Higher-rate springs were fitted to enable additional load to be carried, and the spare wheel was repositioned to a bracket on the front bumper. Stowage facilities were provided on the reinforced front bumper, and inside the vehicle, for jerrycans of fuel and water, and additional stowage bins and lockers were fitted wherever practicable. Armaments included a pair of 7.62mm GPMGs on a coupled mount ahead of the co-driver, with a third GPMG normally stowed beside the driver. A Browning 0.30in machine gun was carried in the rear.

The total number constructed on the 86in chassis may have been just nine, with the first vehicle delivered in April 1955, two more in January 1956, and six in February 1957. A number of 88in Series Is were subsequently converted in a similar manner, remaining in service until 1967, when they were replaced by the long-wheelbase Series IIA 'Pink Panther'.

## Series IIA 'Pink Panther'

In the mid-1960s the SAS decided that the Series I special operations vehicles should be replaced by a long-wheelbase version that could provide additional stowage facilities and permit the operating range to be increased. A document describing the military requirements for 'truck, GS, SAS, ¾ ton, 4x4, Rover 11, FV18064' was drawn up by the regiment in 1964 using experience gained on operations with the existing vehicles. As well as a three-man crew, together with sufficient weaponry for attack and self-defence, the vehicle was required to carry radio communications equipment, and large quantities of fuel, water and other supplies. Working in conjunction with the REME workshops, the regiment produced 27 prototype vehicles, but it was clear that the standard Series II chassis was not up to the task and final development of the vehicle was eventually turned over to FVRDE.

In December 1965, having inspected the existing vehicles, FVRDE issued a new statement of requirements, followed by a detailed specification, the latter finalised in May 1967. Marshalls of Cambridge were asked to construct 72 examples based on the Series IIA chassis, with the first vehicle ready for inspection in August 1968. A number of minor issues were identified for rectification before the first finished vehicles were delivered to the regiment on 2 October 1968, the remainder following during 1969. Universally known as the 'Pink Panther', the vehicle firmly established the style for almost every subsequent special operations vehicle.

As with the earlier SAS prototypes, there were heavy-duty springs and shock absorbers as well as a hydraulic steering damper and one-piece steel wheels mounting 9.00-15 sand tyres. The chassis was reinforced at critical stress points, and welded guards protected the differential housings. Non-essential items – including the doors, sills, windscreen and top – were removed, and the spare wheel was placed in a near-horizontal position on the front bumper, with a folding pannier added to the rear. Twin long-range fuel tanks increased

**LEFT** Bristling with guns, and stowed with every piece of kit that might be required for extended missions behind enemy lines, the Series II-based 'Pink Panther' (FV18064) is probably the most iconic military Land Rover of all time... albeit this example is painted green! *(Tank Museum)*

**ABOVE** The 'Pink Panther' was fitted with heavy-duty springs and shock absorbers and a hydraulic steering damper, and the chassis was reinforced at critical stress points, with welded guards protecting the differential housings. Non-essential items were removed, and twin long-range fuel tanks installed. The standard weapons issue included two 7.62mm GPMGs, a Carl Gustav 84mm recoilless anti-tank gun and four sets of three smoke dischargers. *(RAWHS)*

the fuel load to 100 gallons (454 litres), giving an average operating range of 1,500 miles (2,430km), and there was some rearrangement of components under the bonnet. The passenger seat was fitted to a raised platform, and additional seats were fitted over the rear wheel arches.

Various weapons mounts were fitted, including smoke-grenade launchers and machine-gun mounts, and the standard weapons issue included two 7.62mm GPMGs, a Carl Gustav 84mm recoilless anti-tank gun, and four sets of three electrically-fired smoke dischargers. Other essential equipment included a pair of Larkspur Morse and ground-to-air radio sets, a sun compass, a theodolite and standard magnetic compass. There were stowage facilities for the crew's self-loading rifles (SLRs) in sheet-metal holsters on the sides of the front mudguards, and facilities for stowing ammunition and hand grenades between the front seats and on both sides of the rear compartment. Sand channels and pioneer tools were carried on brackets on the outside of the body, and a machete was stowed behind the rear seat. There were also first-aid facilities, fire

**LEFT** Despite operational losses, the 'Pink Panthers' remained in service for around 20 years, being replaced by the desert patrol vehicle during the late 1980s. Despite the difficulties inherent in tracking down all of the relevant equipment, many are in private hands, often restored to better-than-new condition. *(Warehouse Collection)*

extinguishers and water container racks inside the body. Fully loaded, the vehicle weighed almost 1,000lb (454kg) more than the standard Series IIA.

Despite a tendency to break halfshafts, the vehicles were considered to be reliable and were notably deployed in Belize, Kenya, Northern Ireland and Oman. A standard operating procedure was developed in Oman where the vehicles patrolled in threes, with the leading and rearmost vehicles equipped for the attack or reconnaissance role; the third vehicle carried mechanical spares. The distinctive pink colour also first appeared during the Oman Dhofar operation where it served to conceal the vehicles well against the sun-blasted colour of the desert.

Although there were a few operational losses the 'Pink Panthers' remained in service for around 20 years, eventually being replaced by the Defender 110-based desert patrol vehicles (DPVs) during the late 1980s.

## Desert patrol vehicle

The long-wheelbase Series III was also converted for long-range patrol work, but the leaf-spring suspension made the going tough and in the late 1980s the first of a series of Defender 110 desert patrol vehicles (DPVs)

were produced by Marshalls of Cambridge for British Army service.

Lacking doors, a windscreen, top and frame, the DPV superficially resembled the 'Pink Panther', but was fitted with the distinctive rear body of the civilian high-capacity pickup truck. An external roll cage was fitted behind the front seats and there were additional fuel tanks, as well as generous stowage capacity for additional petrol and water jerrycans, ammunition and personal kit. Two 7.62mm GPMGs were mounted in the rear, with a third pedestal-mounted gun on the scuttle; there were also bumper-mounted smoke

**ABOVE** Fitted with the distinctive rear body of the civilian high-capacity pickup truck and resembling the 'Pink Panthers' in most other respects, the Defender 110 desert patrol vehicles were produced by Marshalls of Cambridge in the late 1980s. *(Tank Museum, Roland Groom)*

**LEFT** A pair of privately-owned DPVs, scarcely visible beneath all of the supplies and personal kit that these vehicles habitually carried. The lead vehicle is armed with a 7.62mm general-purpose machine gun and a MILAN anti-tank missile. *(Phil Royal)*

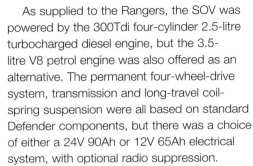

dischargers. Power came from the Buick-derived 3.5-litre V8 petrol engine, and the vehicle was fitted with uprated suspension.

## Special operations vehicle

Although it was also offered to other defence customers, the 'special operations vehicle' (SOV) was originally designed for the US Army Rangers, to provide a rapid-reaction, air-portable all-terrain weapons platform to replace the ageing M151A2. The Rangers had been impressed by the performance of the British Army's Defenders during the liberation of Kuwait, and in 1991 had approached Rover with an outline specification for a similar vehicle. Like the DPV, the Rangers' SOV (sometimes referred to as the RSOV) was based on the long-wheelbase Defender 110. The first example was seen in public at the 1992 Eurosatory Show in Paris, and the Rangers took delivery of 60 examples during 1993.

As supplied to the Rangers, the SOV was powered by the 300Tdi four-cylinder 2.5-litre turbocharged diesel engine, but the 3.5-litre V8 petrol engine was also offered as an alternative. The permanent four-wheel-drive system, transmission and long-travel coil-spring suspension were all based on standard Defender components, but there was a choice of either a 24V 90Ah or 12V 65Ah electrical system, with optional radio suppression.

The bodywork lacked doors, windscreen and top, but for the first time there was a combined roll bar and weapons mount. Suggested armaments included a pair of Boeing 30mm ASP-30 machine guns mounted in tandem at the rear, together with a third machine gun on the scuttle alongside the driver. The vehicle could also mount a 40mm grenade launcher, 50mm or 81mm mortar, 0.50in heavy machine gun, AT-4 Stinger missile or the Carl Gustav 84mm recoilless rifle, the last generally referred to as the 'Ranger anti-tank weapon system' (RAWS). There were additional stowage facilities for ammunition, fuel, water and other tools and equipment.

## Rapid deployment vehicle

Developed in conjunction with Longline and Ricardo Special Vehicles, the 'multi-role combat vehicle' (MRCV) was first seen at the British Army Equipment Exhibition (BAEE) in 1993. Although the demonstrator was based on the short-wheelbase Defender 90 chassis, users could also specify the Defender 110 or 130. The MRCV was subsequently renamed the 'rapid deployment vehicle' (RDV), and the option of using the Defender 130 chassis was discontinued. Two RDV versions were produced – one as a three-seater vehicle with a low-profile rear body and superstructure to allow stowage inside a CH-47 or CH-53E helicopter, without dismantling; the other fitted with a normal-height superstructure to accommodate an additional rear-facing weapons post.

The rear body was of modular construction, allowing easy conversion to suit a specific role, including personnel or cargo carrier, MILAN anti-tank vehicle, or a weapons platform using either a pedestal or a multi-purpose 360° ring mount on the roll bar that could be used

ABOVE **Introduced at the British Army Equipment Exhibition in 1993, the MRCV was originally based on the short-wheelbase Defender 90; users could also specify the Defender 110 or 130, although the use of the latter was eventually discontinued. The vehicle was subsequently renamed as the 'rapid deployment vehicle'.** *(Land Rover Limited)*

to equip the vehicle with a 40mm grenade launcher, GIAT 20mm cannon, L1A1 0.50in Browning heavy machine gun or 7.62mm GPMG. Pedestal mounts could also be fitted to the scuttle, or to the rear, for an 0.50in Browning, 40mm grenade launcher or GIAT 20mm cannon; a 7.62mm GPMG could be mounted anywhere on the roll cage. A lock-out system could be fitted to the suspension to improve stability during firing. In the cargo role, the rear cargo area was designed to accept a palletised load, and there was a large rear bustle that provided additional stowage facilities. As with the SOV, users could choose between a 65Ah 12V electrical system or single or twin 24V 50Ah alternators. Optional radio-suppression facilities were also available.

None of the modifications compromised the vehicle's ability to carry out general service duties.

## Weapons mount

Initially there seems to have been some reluctance to employ the Land Rover as a weapons mount, perhaps because it was seen as 'fragile'. However, by the time the Defender appeared it was clear that the Land Rover was

able to accommodate a range of weapons, with little modification beyond installing the chosen weapons system in the rear, and providing a suitable seat for the gunner and stowage facilities for ammunition.

Examples of weapons to be found on the Land Rover include post-, ring- and cradle-mounted 7.62mm machine guns, in both single and twin configuration; 0.50in machine gun; 12.7mm Gatling gun; 25mm or 30mm cannon; 40mm grenade launcher; and 50mm and 81mm mortar. Anti-tank weapons have been described separately (see page 65), but there is also sufficient space in the rear compartment

ABOVE **The RDV was produced in two versions – a three-seater vehicle with a low-profile body and superstructure to allow transport by helicopter, and a normal-height superstructure that was able to accommodate an additional rear-facing weapons post.** *(MoD)*

BELOW **The Ricardo WMIK consists essentially of a combined roll cage and weapons mount, together with a package of other upgrades, that could be retro-fitted to the Wolf XD Defender, or any other Land Rover that had been upgraded by the installation of reinforced outriggers and roll-cage mounts. The gun here is an 0.50in heavy machine gun.** *(Ian Young)*

for the Defender to be used as a transporter-
launcher for a variety of anti-aircraft weapons,
including the Bofors RBS-70 anti-aircraft
missile, the Thales Air Defence Javelin surface-
to-air missile in its triple LML ('lightweight
multiple launcher') configuration, and the later
Starburst (Javelin S15) anti-aircraft missile.

## Weapons mount installation kit (WMIK)

The 'weapons mount installation kit' was
designed to allow a Defender or Wolf XD to
act as a weapons platform or reconnaissance
vehicle, and to be readily adapted from one role
to another. The development of the kit – which
consists essentially of a combined roll cage
and weapons mount, together with a package
of other upgrades – originated with the 1989
Longline (Cobra) light strike vehicle that was
used by the SAS during the liberation of Kuwait.
Soon after the acquisition of Longline by the
Shoreham-based engineering company Ricardo
Special Vehicles in 1993, Ricardo and Land
Rover agreed on a partnership arrangement
to exploit the WMIK concept. For their part,
Land Rover immediately started to market the
WMIK-equipped MRCV (or RDV, as it later
became) as a standard variation of the so-called

Dating from 2009, this is described
as the 'theatre entry standard' (TES)
R-WMIK, with *appliqué* composite
armour attached to the roll cage.
*(Ian Young)*

'core military' Defender range, whilst Ricardo continued development work.

In early 1998, the British Army took delivery of a WMIK prototype that could be retro-fitted to the Wolf XD Defender or any other Land Rover that had been upgraded by the installation of reinforced outriggers and roll-cage mounts. A trials programme was initiated that led to the MoD issuing a contract for 135 kits to modify existing production vehicles. Within three weeks of the delivery of the first kits in 1999 modified vehicles were in service in Sierra Leone, and to date the British Army has put around 300 WMIK-equipped Land Rovers into service.

Ricardo's original kit is now described as the O-WMIK, although the DERA swing-arm gun mount was replaced by Ricardo's slewing ring in 2002. In mid-2005 the kit was upgraded to become the E-WMIK, with the addition of belly protection plates designed to resist mine blast. From the beginning of 2006 other modifications allowed the gross vehicle weight to be increased from 3.35 to 3.5 tonnes. The current designations are R-WMIK and R-WMIK+, both having additional composite armour in the form of a tub mounted directly on the chassis, on to which the original body panels are refitted. The R-WMIK+ also includes automotive upgrades,

including a new transmission. In 2007 Ricardo announced that a fleet of 200 WMIK-equipped Defenders were being returned for a major upgrade that included significant enhancements to crew-protection systems, as well as an increase in vehicle payload by re-engineering the chassis and suspension systems.

Ricardo has also produced a range of optional WMIK supplementary modules, including infrared lighting systems, lightweight high-back seating systems, snorkel, a hybrid 12/24V electrical system, and wider alloy wheels, the last developed as a result of experience in Afghanistan. WMIK can also be adapted to suit other types of vehicle.

**LEFT** Although not often seen on standard military Land Rovers, smoke-grenade launchers provide an easy method of laying down a smoke screen to allow a vehicle to withdraw unseen or to confuse an enemy as to its true intentions.
*(Phil Royal)*

**BELOW** WMIK-equipped Defenders continue to be deployed wherever it is felt that an open-topped vehicle offers tactical advantage. However, the weight of the kit and the associated upgrades is felt to now be at the limit of the Land Rover chassis' capabilities, and it is unlikely that there will be further significant upgrades.
*(MoD)*

'Tough and versatile, the Land Rover can be seen almost anywhere... often in places where vehicles of any kind are simply not expected... and for over 30 years Land Rovers have been used because no other vehicle will do the particular job.'

**Land Rover Limited sales leaflet**
1982

*Chapter Five*

# Specialised vehicles

With its simple construction, rugged suspension and reputation for reliability, the Land Rover chassis became something of a favourite with third-party companies anxious to prove that there were military applications for 'the world's most versatile vehicle' that even Rover had not imagined. In this manner, Solihull's finest had grown third and fourth axles, been given tracks for extra mobility and been bodied as an armoured car.

**OPPOSITE** Surely the ultimate Land Rover conversion, the tracked Cuthbertson combined low ground pressure with excellent mobility... plus an unrivalled ability to see over hedges! *(British Leyland plc)*

# Armoured vehicles

### Defender 110 APC

Marketed by both Land Rover and Otokar, the Defender 110 armoured personnel carrier (APC) – described by Otokar as the armoured personnel vehicle (APV) – was designed for use by military, paramilitary and security forces, and was constructed around a welded-steel hull able to resist 7.62mm NATO ball ammunition at point-blank range. Glass-fibre reinforced plates were fitted to the underbelly areas and there was armoured glazing with polycarbonate anti-spall liners, optional firing ports, and a small rotating turret mounting a 7.62mm machine gun. The cab provided accommodation for two men, with a further six in the rear. Power was provided by the standard four-cylinder 300Tdi turbocharged diesel engine driving all four wheels through a five-speed manual gearbox and two-speed transfer case. Run-flat tyres were fitted as standard.

### Glover Webb APV and Hornet

In 1983 Glover Webb produced an armoured patrol vehicle based on the Defender 110. Described as 'a highly-mobile non-aggressive armoured personnel carrier with good anti-ballistic properties and a low profile', it was aimed at military and paramilitary forces and was intended for duties such as internal security or riot-control, airfield perimeter control, escort duties, etc.

The vehicle consisted of an eight-man welded armoured-steel hull, with windscreen and side windows of 35mm multi-layer laminated glass with a polycarbonate anti-spall liner. Glass-fibre composites were used to provide grenade and blast protection to the floor, and there was an additional belly plate under the cab area that also protected the explosion-proof fuel tank. There were twin access doors at the rear, and gun ports and additional vision blocks could be fitted if required. The conversion was fully approved by Land Rover and parts' commonality was said to be over 90 per cent.

Subsequently the company also produced a lighter armoured vehicle known

as Hornet, suitable for commando and reconnaissance operations.

## Hotspur Dragoon

Hotspur Armoured Products of Neath demonstrated the Dragoon 6484 armoured personnel carrier at the British Army Equipment Exhibition in 1984. The vehicle was based on the Defender 110 chassis, fitted with an additional powered axle to give a choice of a 6x6 or 6x4 drive-line, and mounting an angular steel-armoured hull that enclosed the engine compartment and provided accommodation for 12 troops in the rear and a crew of two in the cab. The floor was protected against mine and grenade attacks, and the multi-layer laminated glass windscreen and side windows included an anti-spall polycarbonate layer; armoured shutters could be lifted over the windows for maximum protection. A light turret or machine gun hatch could be fitted over the rear compartment.

At the time of launch the company was said to also be considering the production of ambulance and communications variants.

## Hotspur Sandringham

Developed as a private venture, the Sandringham APC was first seen at the June 1980 BAEE. The prototype had completed a trials' programme by early 1981, and production started the following year.

The vehicle was derived from the Sandringham Six (S6), a conversion of the V8-powered Series III Stage One, and was able to accommodate eight fully-equipped troops in the rear compartment, seated on longitudinal benches, together with a crew of two in the cab. The welded hull was constructed from super-hard opaque steel armour, and the floor was protected against mine fragments and grenades. Armour was also used to protect the engine compartment and radiator, and the wheels were equipped with run-flat bands to allow limited operation on a deflated tyre. Access to the cab was provided by hinged doors with large vision windows of composite glass and plastic construction, with polycarbonate anti-spall screens; hinged armoured screens were also available for the windscreen and side windows, and there were

six firing ports with vision blocks. Access to the rear compartment was provided by a pair of hinged doors.

A choice of wheelbase lengths was available, at 125in and 139in, with the vehicles identified as the S6 and S6E respectively. Other body variants included a field ambulance, command and communications vehicle, long-distance patrol vehicle and fuel or water tanker. A commander's cupola could be installed in the roof at the rear, designed to mount a GPMG; it was also possible to adapt the vehicle as a gun tractor or weapons/missile platform.

## MACOSA BMU-2

In 1983 the Spanish heavy engineering company MACOSA (Material y Construcciones SA) constructed a prototype four-wheeled armoured car, designated BMU-2, on the chassis of the long-wheelbase Santana. Weighing 7,260lb (3,300kg), the vehicle was powered by the Santana six-cylinder diesel engine producing 92bhp from 3,429cc.

**ABOVE** The Glover Webb Hornet was a light armoured vehicle suitable for commando and reconnaissance operations. *(Tank Museum, Roland Groom)*

**LEFT** Derived from the Sandringham Six (S6) conversion of the Series III Stage One, the Sandringham APC was launched at the British Army Equipment Exhibition in June 1980, with production starting in 1982. The armoured hull provided accommodation for eight fully-equipped troops in the rear compartment, seated on longitudinal benches, together with a two-man crew. *(Warehouse Collection)*

It was planned that there might be ambulance, command car and communications variants, but there was no series production.

## Otokar *Akrep*

The Turkish Otokar firm also offered armoured Land Rovers for military, paramilitary and internal security roles, including a 'discreetly armoured station wagon' that was said to resemble a standard Defender 110. The *Akrep* ('Scorpion') lightweight attack/defence vehicle and APC derivatives were more militaristic in appearance, and incorporated Defender automotive components in a heavy-duty armoured body; see page 119. Standard variants included ambulance and workshop vehicles.

## Penman Engineering Skirmisher and Hussar

The Skirmisher and Hussar armoured vehicles were designed by Penman Engineering using the V8-powered Defender 110; the Skirmisher retained the original 4x4 drive-line, whilst

the 6x6 Hussar was fitted with a second driven axle. Intended military and security roles included ambulance, command vehicle, escort or prisoner transport and patrol and reconnaissance duties.

With slightly better ballistic protection than so-called 'non-aggressive' armoured bodies such as the Glover Webb and Hotspur machines, the angular body of the Hussar and Skirmisher were constructed from welded armoured steel. Both vehicles offered similar levels of protection, with windows and the windscreen constructed from multi-layer laminated glass with a polycarbonate anti-spall layer; armoured shutters were also provided. Vision blocks were fitted along each side and in the rear access doors, and all of the doors were constructed to the same ballistic standard as the hull. Floor armour provided protection from mine fragments and grenades, and the engine compartment was also protected. A roof-mounted turret or machine-gun hatch could be fitted.

Hussar was designed to accommodate 12 men in the rear and a two-man crew in the cab, whilst the smaller Skirmisher provided accommodation for eight men in the rear compartment plus a two-man crew.

## Shorland armoured patrol car

The Shorland armoured patrol car was initially produced for the Royal Ulster Constabulary (RUC), although it eventually saw service in locations as far apart as Africa, the Far East, the Middle East and South America. Development work started in 1961 when the RUC was searching for alternatives to the heavy armoured personnel carriers that were in use at that time. A number of military Land Rovers serving in the Province had already been fitted with *appliqué* armour, which suggested that an armoured Land Rover could provide the basis for a well-protected law-enforcement vehicle.

A meeting was convened at the workshops of the Ministry of Home Affairs to consider the viability of mounting an armoured body on a standard Land Rover chassis. A simple design was sketched out by Police Support Officer Ernie Lusty, and a wooden mock-up prepared for demonstration at the meeting. Official go-ahead for the project was given in July 1962, and a mild-steel prototype was constructed

**LEFT** Although their cross-country performance meant that the Shorlands were widely used for border patrols, many were also deployed on the streets of Belfast and Derry/Londonderry. Those vehicles that entered service with the RUC were passed to the Ulster Defence Regiment. *(Warehouse Collection)*

**ABOVE** With development work starting in 1961, the Shorland armoured patrol car was produced for the Royal Ulster Constabulary as an alternative to heavier armoured personnel carriers. Produced in five 'marks', it eventually also saw service Africa, the Far East, the Middle East and South America. *(Tank Museum)*

**RIGHT** A small number of Shorlands have passed into private ownership. This example, believed to be a late-model Defender-based prototype for the Series 5, seems to have acquired a Wolf air intake. *(Simon Thomson)*

**BELOW** Shorland Mk 3 equipped with a pair of Vigilant anti-tank missiles mounted on the sides of a special turret. It was believed that in this form the Shorland would appeal to developing nations seeking a low-cost anti-tank capability. *(Warehouse Collection)*

**RIGHT** Shorland Mk 5 (S53) air-defence vehicle equipped with a multiple Blowpipe missile system. *(Warehouse Collection)*

**ABOVE** Huzar is an armoured patrol vehicle produced by Polish company Marek Pasierbski, using the Defender 130 chassis, to which has been added a third coil-sprung driven axle to give a 6x6 drive-line.
*(Marek Pasierbski)*

during December 1962 and January 1963 in the Ministry's Belfast workshops, using an existing low-mileage long-wheelbase Series II as a donor vehicle. Following some modifications, including the use of a Ferret turret carrying a 0.30in machine gun, the vehicle was put into production by Short Brothers & Harland Limited at their Newtonards factory in County Down, under the name Shorland.

The vehicles started coming off the production line in July 1965, based on the long-wheelbase Series IIA. The first ten examples were delivered to the RUC in the spring of 1966, and a total of some 1,500 vehicles, in five 'marks', had been produced by the time production came to an end in the mid-1990s.

### WZP Huzar

Based on the Defender 130 chassis, with the addition of a third coil-sprung driven axle, Huzar is a 6x6 armoured conversion produced by Polish company Marek Pasierbski in Wroclaw. Although various engines have been used, including the 300Tdi, and Puma Td4, when demonstrated to the Polish Army in 2004 the vehicle was powered by a five-cylinder 2,493cc Td5 engine coupled to a five-speed gearbox. The modular armoured hull was developed by AMZ-Kutno, and although normally open-topped at the rear could be modified to provide overhead protection. Run-flat inserts allowed the vehicle to continue to operate with one or more deflated tyres.

It was planned that the vehicle would eventually be offered in three variants: the A-model, based on the Defender 130; the B-model, derived from the Defender 110;

and the smaller C-model, using the Defender 90 chassis.

## Tracked vehicles

### Centaur half-track

The half-tracked Centaur was a private venture by Laird (Anglesey) Limited, with work starting in 1977. Described by its creators as a 'multi-purpose military vehicle system', it was intended to 'combine the ease of operation of a road vehicle with the tractive performance and off-road capabilities of a track-layer'. The first prototypes appeared in April 1978, and it was anticipated that series production would begin the following year.

The basis of the vehicle was the chassis and cab of the Defender Stage One, complete with the Buick-derived V8 petrol engine, which for this application was tuned to produce 156bhp. A steel subframe was attached at the rear, allowing the axle to be replaced by a shortened version of the track and torsion-bar suspension system of the Alvis Scorpion FV101 CVR(T) (combat vehicle reconnaissance, tracked) range. There was a permanent four-wheel-drive system using a four-speed gearbox and two-speed transfer box, with the lockable centre differential transmitting power equally to the front wheels and the tracks. The tracks were tensioned by a hydraulic ram and there was a single idler wheel at the rear, with no track-return rollers. At the front end the standard Land Rover front axle was suspended on multi-leaf elliptical springs. No steering action was available from the tracks, and changes of direction were handled by the standard Burman recirculating-ball system, without power assistance. The front brakes were the standard drums, whilst at the rear there were inboard discs, each with twin callipers. Although it was at the expense of fuel consumption, top speed on the road was a creditable 50mph (81kph), and the combination of a very low centre of gravity and the traction available ensured a formidable off-road performance. The cost of the vehicle compared favourably to the standard Land Rover and driver-training issues were minimal, but on the downside there was an increased requirement for maintenance.

**RIGHT** Dating from 1977, the Laird Centaur was a three-quarter-track vehicle that combined the chassis of the V8-powered Series III Stage One with a shortened version of the track system from the Alvis CVR(T) family. *(Tank Museum)*

**BELOW** Two pre-production Centaurs were sold to Oman in 1978, and the British Army subjected one example to cold-weather trials in Norway, but the Centaur project was abandoned in 1985 in response to a lack of sales orders. *(Tank Museum)*

In its load-carrying role the vehicle was rated at 3 tons. It was also possible to employ the vehicle as a ten-man personnel carrier, minelayer, recovery vehicle, gun tractor for the Rapier anti-aircraft missile system, or a gun/missile mount. In the last role the Centaur could, typically, be adapted to carry the 106mm recoilless anti-tank gun, Swingfire, MILAN or TOW anti-tank missile system, 20mm anti-aircraft guns, 60mm mortar system or 7.62mm machine guns. A fully-enclosed vehicle was also mocked-up for use as a four-stretcher ambulance or communications vehicle, and Laird announced that a fully-armoured variant would also be made available and could be fitted out as a battlefield ambulance, command vehicle or reconnaissance vehicle, in the last case armed with a small rotating turret mounting a 7.62mm machine gun.

Two pre-production models were sold to Oman in 1978, and the British Army shipped one example to Norway for cold-weather trials. However, despite a lot of interest from overseas,

total production is believed to have amounted to just seven or eight vehicles, and by 1985 escalating development costs and low sales saw the project abandoned.

## Cuthbertson four-track

In the early 1960s James A. Cuthbertson Limited (JAC) of Biggar, Lanarkshire, produced a high-mobility Land Rover conversion for use on soft ground. Consisting of a standard Land Rover chassis bolted to a full-length subframe, the standard road wheels were replaced by sprockets arranged to drive endless nylon/cotton-reinforced steel-cleated rubber tracks, each supported on a pair of solid-tyred bogie wheels. The front bogies provided steering effort through a hydraulic power-assisted system.

All this additional equipment increased the unladen weight of an 88in Land Rover to 5,500lb (2,500kg), but all of the additional weight was low down and the centre of gravity was not unduly compromised. The conversion provided excellent stability combined with good

**ABOVE** Lairds envisaged that the Centaur would form the basis of a family of vehicles, and a mock-up was constructed showing a fully-enclosed hull that could be equipped as a four-stretcher ambulance or communications vehicle. The company also stated that there would be a fully-armoured variant. *(Tank Museum)*

**RIGHT** James A. Cuthbertson Limited devised a way of mounting a standard Land Rover, in this case a Series I, on a subframe in such a way that sprockets attached to the original hubs were coupled to endless nylon/cotton-reinforced steel-cleated rubber tracks, supported on solid-tyred bogie wheels. The vehicle offered high mobility combined with low ground pressure and was ideal for bomb disposal work. *(J.A. Cuthbertson Limited)*

**RIGHT** Alongside a number of Series II/IIA civilian vehicles, Cuthbertson also converted some Series III 'lightweights', with the latter being purchased by the RAF. *(J.A. Cuthbertson Limited)*

performance on soft and marshy ground. Both the War Office and the Air Ministry thought that the vehicle would be ideal for bomb disposal work and a small number of Series Is and Series III 'lightweights' are known to have been supplied to the military in this configuration. Cuthbertson continued to offer the conversion to civilians, and both Series I and Series II vehicles, in both long- and short-wheelbase forms, were converted.

# Multi-wheeled vehicles

### Esarco

Developed by Esarco Limited of Ludgershall, and manufactured by Laird (Anglesey) Limited, the Esarco 8x8 all-terrain vehicle first appeared in the late 1970s. With almost all of the automotive components derived from the Defender 110, including the engine, transmission, axles and suspension, it was aimed at both military and civilian users, and was initially designed for a payload of 1½ tons, but after preliminary testing the manufacturers decided that the payload could be safely increased to 2 tons.

The chassis was constructed from mild steel box-section main members with welded cross-members, and mounted a simple mild steel flat-panelled open-topped forward-control cab making widespread use of Land Rover body fittings. Early Esarcos were powered by the Buick-derived 3.5-litre V8 engine, with the VM Motori 692 six-cylinder diesel engine subsequently offered as an option, and the drive-line consisted of a Land Rover five-speed manual gearbox or an optional three-speed automatic 'box, and a pair of full-time four-wheel-drive Land Rover transfer cases, mounted back to back, each incorporating a lockable differential. The first transfer case was coupled to axles one and three, whilst the second drove axles two and four, allowing the vehicle to be operated either as an 8x8 or an 8x4. The axle differentials were offset, which allowed the propeller shafts to pass over the intervening axles on their way to the appropriate wheels, thus keeping them well out of harm's way. Both the front and rearmost axles were arranged to steer, giving a tight turning circle, and high-flotation 31in (788mm) diameter Goodyear tyres were fitted to keep ground pressure to the minimum. The front and rear axles used hydraulic disc brakes, whilst there were drums on the centre axles. Top speed on the road was in the order of 60–65mph (95–105kph), and a power take-off allowed the vehicle to be operated in conjunction with a powered trailer or for a winch to be fitted.

At the rear the canvas-covered drop-sided cargo body could double as a ten-man troop carrier, and an optional closed body was also offered. Alongside the standard cargo version, other variants either planned or prototyped included a field ambulance, tipper truck, fire-fighter, a weapons platform designed to carry, for example, the Rapier surface-to-air missile system or an Oerlikon 20mm anti-aircraft cannon, and a helicopter field service vehicle fitted with working platforms either side of an open load-carrying work area. The vehicle was also trialled as an aircraft tug and fire-fighter, and there was a planned steel-hulled amphibious version. An armoured variant was marketed by Glover Webb under the name Glover-Esarco.

By 1988 the original 8x8 had been joined

**RIGHT** The Esarco 8x8 all-terrain vehicle was developed by Esarco Limited of Ludgershall, and employed automotive components from the Defender 110, including the engine, transmission, axles and suspension. It first appeared in the late 1970s and was put into production by Laird (Anglesey) Limited, aimed at both military and civilian users. *(Warehouse Collection)*

by a 6x6 flat-platform variant developed as a contender for the British Army's all-terrain mobile platform (ATMP), a role that eventually went to the Fairey (later Alvis) Supacat. The Esarco 6x6 equally borrowed heavily from the Defender 110 and was powered by either the standard 3.5-litre V8 petrol engine or the 300Tdi four-cylinder 2.5-litre turbocharged diesel. The loss of one axle reduced the payload to 1 ton, but with reduced performance the vehicle was said to be able to carry 1½ tons.

MWG All-Terrain Vehicles Limited of Chertsey had taken on the marketing of the vehicles by the early 1990s, and there had been considerable redesign and improvement. The Land Rover engines had been replaced by the Perkins Phaser 110T, but the Land Rover five-speed manual gearbox was retained for the 6x6, the 8x8 being fitted with a Chrysler three-speed automatic gearbox. The chassis was redesigned as a robust four-box section, and the 8x8 was fitted with a four-door Land Rover crew-cab structure with a built-in roll cage.

*Jane's Combat Support Equipment* reported that the original 8x8 was in service with the Royal Air Force (although this is likely to have been a single trials vehicle) and with the armies of Saudi Arabia and Zimbabwe. Six examples of the 6x6 variant were in service with Portuguese paratroop forces, where it was used to tow a 120mm mortar and carry a crew of six.

## Sandringham 6

Constructed by Hotspur Cars Limited, Sandringham 6 was a 6x6 conversion of the Stage One, offering excellent load-carrying and off-road performance through a combination of V8 engine, permanent six-wheel drive, and lockable centre differential. The rights to the design were sold to Penman Engineering in the mid-1980s, when the vehicle reappeared as

the Hotspur One Fifty, based on Defender 110 components. Rated at 3 tons and powered by the 3.5-litre V8 petrol engine (the 2.5-litre four-cylinder turbocharged diesel engine was offered initially but was subsequently dropped), the vehicle was said to be suitable for applications such as fire rescue, command vehicle, long-range desert patrol vehicle, light weapons platform, gun tractor, maintenance vehicle, helicopter servicing vehicle and explosive ordnance disposal (EOD).

The conversion was fully approved by Land Rover and there was over 90 per cent commonality of parts. At least one example was trialled by the British Army as a gun tractor.

**LEFT** In June 1988 a Defender 110-based Esarco 6x6 was offered to the British Army for the all-terrain mobile platform role, and it was trialled in Singapore. However, the contract was awarded to Fairey (later Alvis) with their Supacat. *(Simon Thomson)*

**LEFT** The Sandringham 6 was constructed by Hotspur Cars Limited, and was a 6x6 conversion of the Series III Stage One. One of the roles envisaged for it was that of long-range desert patrol vehicle. The rights to the design were sold to Penman Engineering in the mid-1980s. *(Tank Museum)*

'...mphibians may be used in an assault to land ...ersonnel and supporting arms where beach ...onditions or coral off-shore make it difficult ... impossible to use landing craft or where the ...umber of landing craft that can be transported ... the scene of operations is inadequate.'

...e War Office;
...mphibious warfare handbook 9C
...57

# Chapter Six

# Experimental military vehicles

One of the advantages of being funded by the taxpayer is that the money never really runs out, and whilst this can have its downsides it also means that the military is never afraid to try something new simply on the grounds of cost. Over the years the Land Rover has been trialled for various aborted specialised roles, as well as being subjected to all sorts of mechanical indignities, ranging from the use of hover fans in an attempt to make it fly, to the use of huge doughnut-shaped tyres that enable it to skim across water.

OPPOSITE The 'one-ton amphibious Land Rover' (OTAL) was developed for the Australian Defence Force but never entered series production. (Phil Royal)

## Series I command car

Having already taken a close look at the Tickford station wagon, in 1951–52 the War Office asked Land Rover to produce a prototype for a military command car. The vehicle was constructed on either the standard 80in chassis or a prototype of the 86in chassis that was in development, and was described in Rover files as an 'army staff car'. The body was of full-width four-door design, somewhat utilitarian in appearance, with accommodation for six men – two in the front, two on a rear-facing bench and two more on inward-facing seats at the extreme rear, all of the rear seats being grouped around a map table. To increase versatility the backrest to the rear bench seat could be swung across to provide a forward-facing seat.

The flat-sided body was wider than the standard Land Rover front end, with the scuttle projecting by 2–3in (50–75mm) on either side. Surviving photographs show that there was sliding glass fitted into all four doors, and a one-piece, fixed, rubber-glazed windscreen. There was a single door at the rear, on which was mounted a large metal stowage bin, and there was a luggage rack on the roof reached by means of a step on the left-hand rear body panel.

The prototype was pitched head-to-head against a mock-up heavy utility vehicle on the FV1600 series Humber 1-ton chassis, but there was no series production. The prototype was disposed of in 1962.

A similar experimental four-door command vehicle was constructed on the 107in pickup chassis in 1955–56 but again there were no further vehicles built, and from mid-1955 the War Office started to purchase small numbers of standard station wagons for this role.

## Australian OTAL military amphibian

In 1965 an experimental amphibious Land Rover was produced for the Australian Defence Force. Identified as OTAL ('one-ton amphibious Land Rover'), the vehicle was built using as many standard Land Rover Series IIA components as possible, and also adopted the non-standard 97in wheelbase previously seen on FV18061.

The high-waisted body was designed to provide maximum freeboard, and consisted of

an engine compartment attached to a pair of watertight aluminium units. The first of these housed the driver and two passengers, with access available via shallow drop-down doors; a mechanical winch was carried on the front apron. The rear unit provided the cargo area. The engine and transmission were waterproofed and the vents and breathers were placed above the waterline; a short snorkel protruded through the bonnet on the right-hand side and the exhaust pipe was extended to roof level. The front mudguards were foam-filled to act as buoyancy units, and closed-cell polyurethane foam was injected into the chassis sections and the under-floor area.

Trials were carried out in February 1966 and the cross-country performance was described as being 'up to normal Land Rover standards'. It was a different story in the water, where, at least initially, the wheels provided the sole means of progress. The addition of some form of 'deflector' fitted at or near each wheel station was subsequently said to allow the vehicle 'to cope with most inland water flows'.

There were no subsequent orders, and the lone prototype was shipped back to the UK, where it remained for a while at Land Rover's off-road centre before becoming part of the Dunsfold Collection.

## 'Big lightweight'

Rover produced what was virtually a larger version of the standard military 'lightweight' as a private venture in the mid- to late-1960s. The wheelbase was 110in, and the vehicle offered a ¾-ton payload and increased power, and had the ability to be used with the Scottorn Bushmaster 1-ton powered trailer to give a choice of 6x6, 6x4 and 6x2 drive-line configurations. Often described as the 'big lightweight', the vehicle shared a similar design approach to the smaller machine, with a wide flat-fronted grille, high cutaway mudguards front and rear, and flat-panelled demountable two-door open bodywork that could be stripped to reduce the overall weight to 3,800lb (1,728kg) for air-portability.

Power came from the 3-litre six-cylinder 110bhp petrol engine of the P5 and P5B saloon car, used in combination with a four-speed gearbox and two-speed transfer box driving heavy-duty, wide-track ENV axles borrowed from the civilian forward-control models, suspended on semi-elliptical springs, front and rear. Tyres were 9.00-16 rather than the more normal 7.50-16 items. The trailer was driven via a second transfer box at the rear of the chassis.

One example was displayed at the exhibition of British military vehicles at the Fighting Vehicles Research & Development Establishment in 1966, whilst a second was shown at Aldershot Army Day in 1968. By 1970 these two vehicles had been submitted for what were described as 'performance assessment trials', carried out at Hankley Common near Aldershot. The vehicle was considered – but subsequently rejected – for the role that was eventually filled by the forward-control '101'.

## 1½-ton forward control

During 1965 both Austin and Rover submitted forward-control prototypes to the FVRDE to meet a requirement for a '1½-ton GS load carrier'; Bedford and Commer also produced normal-control vehicles for the same role. The vehicles were subsequently

**FAR LEFT** Consisting of an engine compartment attached to a pair of watertight aluminium units, OTAL's high-waisted body was designed to provide maximum freeboard. A powerful mechanical winch was mounted on the front bumper to assist in self-recovery.
*(Phil Royal)*

**ABOVE** Rated at ¾ ton, the so-called 'big lightweight' was a private venture dating from the mid- to late-1960s. It was designed to be used in conjunction with the Scottorn Bushmaster 1-ton powered trailer to give a choice of 6x6, 6x4 and 6x2 drive-line configurations, and like the standard 'lightweight', the flat-panelled two-door open bodywork could be stripped to reduce the weight for air-portability.
*(Tank Museum)*

40mph (64kph), with 15mph (24kph) available across country.

None of the four submissions was selected for production and the role was never fulfilled in the envisaged form.

## Portuguese Army 1-ton wader

**BELOW** Although the 1½-ton prototype was not selected for production, it was not broken-up and later served as a recovery vehicle for the Rover Engineering Department, before passing to the BMIHT museum at Gaydon, where it is affectionately referred to as 'Buttercup'. *(Warehouse Collection)*

demonstrated at the 1966 Exhibition of Military Vehicles held at FVRDE's Chertsey site.

Bearing a passing resemblance to the civilian Series IIB, Land Rover's prototype mounted a widened version of the centre section of the Series II cab, with a sharply cut-off short nose and a cargo body designed to accept a standard 1-ton container. Power came from a Perkins 6.354 six-cylinder diesel engine, producing 105bhp from 5.8 litres, driving all four wheels through a five-speed gearbox and two-speed transfer box. The wheelbase was extended to 112in and the unladen weight of the completed vehicle was 7,460lb (3,390kg). Maximum speed on the road was quoted at

In around 1971–72 Land Rover produced a 1-ton prototype for a possible Portuguese Army contract for a vehicle designed to ferry cargo to the shore from ships moored in shallow water. Based on a standard 109in diesel-engined chassis, the custom-built cab resembled that fitted to the standard 'lightweight', whilst the fixed-sided open rear body, which was probably constructed in Portugal, was designed to accept two standard Portuguese pallets or could be equipped with wooden bench seats for six men.

The vehicle was shipped to Sociedade Electro-Mecanica de Automoveis Ltda (SEMAL), who assembled Land Rovers from CKD kits in Lisbon. Despite being trialled in Portugal the bid was unsuccessful, and the unique vehicle was returned to Britain before being disposed of in 1978. It has survived in the Dunsfold Collection.

## Llama

To coincide with the appearance of a completely new vehicle at the British Army Equipment Exhibition in June 1986, Rover issued a press release describing what came to be known as the Llama – although, in fact, the vehicle was never given an official name. Work had started on the project during 1985 with a view to providing a more modern and 'civilised' vehicle rated at 2 tons to replace the ageing military forward-control '101' – for which, incidentally, the Ministry of Defence had turned down Rover's offer of a comprehensive midlife rebuild at a fraction of the cost of new trucks.

Bearing little resemblance to any contemporary Land Rover, it was constructed around a heavy-duty steel ladder chassis, with a unique three-man tilt cab consisting of glass-fibre composite outer panels bonded to an aluminium tubular space frame. Mechanical components were derived from the Defender 110, with power provided by the Buick-derived V8 petrol engine coupled to the standard permanent all-wheel-drive transmission, consisting of a five-speed gearbox and two-speed transfer case with centre lockable differential. A centre power take-off was included to drive an under-floor winch.

**ABOVE LEFT** Dating from 1971–72, the 1-ton 'Portuguese wader' was designed to ferry cargo to the shore from ships moored in shallow water. The prototype was based on a standard 109in diesel-engined chassis, to which was fitted a custom-built cab and locally-constructed fixed-sided open rear body. *(Warehouse Collection)*

**ABOVE** Following trials in Portugal, the prototype 'wader' was deemed unsatisfactory and was returned to Britain. The vehicle was disposed of in 1978 and has survived in the Dunsfold Collection. *(Warehouse Collection)*

**BELOW** 'Project Llama' was initiated in 1985 with a view to providing a modern replacement for the ageing 'FC 101'. Rated at 2 tons, and powered by the V8 petrol engine, Llama prototypes were constructed on a new heavy-duty chassis, mounting a unique tilt cab comprising glass-fibre composite outer panels bonded to an aluminium tubular space frame. *(Tank Museum, Roland Groom)*

**ABOVE** Eleven Llama prototypes were built and equipped with a variety of bodies, including a canvas-covered aluminium-alloy fixed-side cargo vehicle, a demountable glass-fibre DROPS (demountable rack offload and pickup system), a box van that was mocked-up as both an ambulance and communications vehicle, a gun tractor, and a missile launcher. The project was cancelled in 1988. *(Tank Museum, Roland Groom)*

The axles were heavy-duty Salisbury units suspended on coil springs, and the steering was power-assisted. There was a choice of 12V and 24V electrical systems.

During 1986–87 Rover built 11 prototypes and a single production vehicle, with a second production vehicle assembled from parts during 1998. The vehicles were fitted with a range of typical bodies including a canvas-covered aluminium-alloy fixed-side cargo body, a demountable glass-fibre 'pod' that could be loaded and unloaded from the chassis using what was effectively a smaller version of the Multilift DROPS (demountable rack offload and pickup system), a box van that was mocked-up as both an ambulance and communications vehicle, a gun tractor, and a missile launcher. The prototypes were submitted to the Defence Evaluation & Research Agency, where they were subjected to off-road driving, stability, cold-weather, load-carrying and endurance/performance tests, in some cases being directly compared to 4x4 and 6x6 forward-control trucks produced by Stonefield. Several defects came to light, the most serious of which was that the combination of relatively compliant coil-spring suspension and a high centre of gravity resulted in poor stability over rough ground when fully laden.

The Llama project was cancelled in 1988 when it became clear that there would be no Ministry of Defence orders.

## Challenger

Land Rover's Challenger project dates from early 1990s and was an attempt at creating a range of military utility vehicles based on the Discovery chassis. During its early stages the project was referred to within Land Rover as Defender II, and just two prototypes are believed to have been constructed, one bodied as a general service pickup, the other as a station wagon. The prototypes were powered by a militarised version of the 200Tdi turbocharged diesel unit originally developed under the code name Gemini. The transmission was a four-speed fully-automatic ZF unit. Some interior items were borrowed from the Discovery, but much of the bodywork was hand-made.

The vehicle was shown to the Ministry of Defence, and although the project did not proceed in this guise some of the thinking and technology resurfaced on the Wolf Defender XD. The project was abandoned in 1991, but one of the prototypes has survived.

## Experimental conversions

Once the Land Rover had become established as the standard British Army utility vehicle examples were often singled out for one-off or limited production experimental work.

### Rolls-Royce-engined Series I

In May 1949 33 examples of the 80in wheelbase Series I were fitted with the Rolls-Royce B40 engine that was destined

**RIGHT** Dating from the early 1990s, Challenger was another stillborn project, this time aimed at creating a range of military utility vehicles based on the Discovery chassis. Two prototypes are believed to have been constructed, one of which is now in private hands. *(Simon Thomson)*

for eventual use in the Austin Champ. The modification, which was carried out by Hudson Motors, entailed extending the wheelbase to 81in, stiffening the front springs to better support the weight of the engine, modifying two of the chassis cross-members and fitting a new bell housing and propeller shaft. Together with the new engine, these modifications added some 220lb (100kg) to the weight of the vehicle.

It has often been suggested that the War Office was interested in whether or not the Land Rover could be powered by the standardised Rolls-Royce engine, examples of which were also to be found in the Humber 1-ton truck, Saladin armoured car, Ferret scout car and Saracen armoured personnel carrier, amongst others. However, the truth is that the Land Rover was simply being used as a test bed, since the development of the Champ was continuing to drag on.

## Conversion to diesel power

Land Rover did not provide a diesel-powered option until 1957. However, diesel power had a strong following in the agricultural community, and the Turner Manufacturing Company of Wolverhampton had been marketing a conversion kit since 1953, using either the company's L40 engine, a 2-litre supercharged two-cylinder unit, or the L60, which was a three-cylinder unit with a displacement of 3 litres. In 1957 FVRDE asked Turner to install an L60 unit in a 109in wheelbase Series II, and subsequently put the vehicle through a series of trials. No series purchases followed.

The Irish Defence Force also undertook an experiment into the advantages of converting to diesel power when, in the 1980s, they fitted diesel engines to a number of previously petrol-powered Defender 110 vehicles, using kits supplied by Solihull. The chosen engine was the 200Tdi, a four-cylinder turbocharged unit producing 107bhp from a capacity of 2,495cc, and the result should have been identical to factory-produced vehicles with the same specification, but with the original gearboxes remaining in place the gear ratios did not suit the power curve of the engine, and the conversion – which was reported to be slow and noisy – was not considered to be a success.

## Independent front suspension

Opinions differ regarding the design of suspension for off-road vehicles. Supporters of independent suspension hold that by allowing individual movement at each wheel the vehicle stands the best chance of maintaining traction at all four corners, since it is less likely that one or more wheels will have been lifted off the ground. However, those who favour the live-axle set-up argue that the advantages that independent suspension confers are more than outweighed by variations in axle clearance that occur as the vehicle rolls and pitches in response to the terrain – reduced ground clearance, of course, increases the chances of getting stuck on rocky or heavily undulating ground.

**ABOVE In May 1949 33 examples of the 80in Series I were fitted with the Rolls-Royce B40 engine that was destined for eventual use in the Austin Champ. At the end of the trials period at least one example was converted to a royal review vehicle.** *(Warehouse Collection)*

**LEFT Under-bonnet view showing the Rolls-Royce B40 engine in place. There was never any long-term intention to equip the Land Rover with the Rolls-Royce engine; the vehicles were simply acting as mobile test beds.** *(Warehouse Collection)*

By tradition Land Rovers have always been equipped with live axles and leaf springs, whilst the Austin Champ had independent suspension using longitudinal torsion bars. This at least partly explains why the Champ offered superior off-road performance, and in 1955–56 – in an effort, perhaps, to improve the off-road performance of the Land Rover – FVRDE asked Rover to develop an experimental independent front suspension (IFS) layout for the 86in Series I.

The live front axle was replaced by a rigidly mounted differential unit, and the chassis was modified to allow the front hubs to be carried on twin wishbone arms. A square laminated torsion bar was mounted parallel to, and below the chassis frame on each side, using a substantial bracket ahead of the body outrigger. At its front end the torsion bar was linked to the wishbone. Large, double-acting telescopic shock absorbers were fitted at each wheel station and rubber conical bump stops were fitted to provide a progressive spring rate at the upper limit of suspension travel. This arrangement gave a total movement at each front wheel of 5.4in (137mm) from full bump to full rebound, with the shock absorber being the limiting factor. Modifications were made to the steering linkage to accommodate the greater movement of the wheel station. A second steering relay unit was attached to the chassis on the nearside, and the long drag link which normally transfers the steering action from the nearside to offside wheels was omitted. The two relay units were connected by a short tie rod, and similar tie rods conveyed the steering action to each front wheel. At the rear the standard springs were replaced by dual-rate units.

Ground clearance under the front axle shield was 9.75in (248mm), and under the torsion bar bracket 9in (229mm), so the minimum 8.5in (216mm) ground clearance of the standard Land Rover was not compromised. However, the changes increased the unladen weight of the vehicle by about 10 per cent , to 2,912lb (1,325kg).

The IFS Land Rover was trialled against a Champ and a standard Land Rover with somewhat mixed results. Over a cross-country course the modified Land Rover achieved an average speed of 17.6mph (28.5kph) when driven at the 'maximum safe speed compatible with crew comfort', compared to 19mph (31kph) for the Champ and 17mph (27.5kph) for the leaf-sprung Land Rover. On the rough-road course the equivalent speeds were all within a whisker of 35mph (57kph), with the Champ just having the edge. Finally the vehicles were run at 10, 20 and 30mph (16, 32 and 48kph) on *pavé* and on the punishing 'number 2' suspension course with its raised 1–1.5in (25–38mm) concrete ribs. Here the IFS Land Rover offered slightly better comfort than the standard model at 10mph (16kph), but steering wander and comfort deteriorated at 20mph (32kph) and improved slightly at 30mph (50kph). The Champ behaved in much the same way, but the rear suspension of all three performed poorly when the vehicles were travelling at 30mph (50kph).

Braking trials showed that the braking performance was not compromised by the IFS set-up and there was no undue 'nosing down' of the Land Rover under emergency braking. The steering of the IFS Land Rover was said to be noticeably lighter than that of the standard vehicle on roads, but the more heavily-damped steering of the leaf-sprung model was preferred on the cross-country, suspension and rough-road courses. With its rack-and-pinion steering and all-round independent suspension, the Champ was said to be 'superior to the other two vehicles under all conditions of the test'.

Surprisingly, it seems that there was 'little improvement in the riding or handling characteristics of the Land Rover with independent front suspension when compared to the standard model', and at the end of the trials the Land Rover was returned to the manufacturer. To this day, 'proper' Land Rovers retain a live-axle set-up.

## High-flotation wheels

During the early 1950s the prolific Austrian inventor Nicholas Straussler had experimented with oversized wheels fitted with low-pressure high-flotation tyres. These were designed to allow a vehicle to cross marshland and shallow water obstacles by making the wheels virtually float on the surface; propulsion in the water was provided by bars across the tread face and scoops on the sides. Straussler's wheels were trialled on the Series I, as well as on Jeeps and Champs, but proved a little too unwieldy for practical use – not to mention more than filling the entire cargo bay of the vehicle in question when not in use.

In the early 1970s there was another round of trials with a similar design, this time using

a Series II fitted with huge low-pressure, slick 'doughnut' tyres which, again, were intended to provide both buoyancy and propulsion. Although the tyres enabled the vehicle to literally walk on water the trials were eventually abandoned, and this project too never reached fruition.

High-flotation tyres were revived yet again, albeit in a slightly different form, in the mid-1980s when

**ABOVE AND LEFT** In the mid-1980s Gloster Saro modified a number of 'lightweights' for use in the Falkland Islands. The modifications included a high-level exhaust, oversized Goodyear Wrangler dumper tyres, extended wheel arches, a new front bumper and a steering damper. (Warehouse Collection)

Gloster Saro modified a number of 'lightweights' by fitting 15½in Goodyear Wrangler dumper tyres for use in the Falkland Islands, where the terrain was frequently soft, wet and marshy. Other modifications included a high-level exhaust, a new bumper designed to carry a spare wheel, a steering damper, and extended wheel arches.

## Hover Rover

Although air-cushion or hovercraft vehicles had first appeared as far back as 1915, it wasn't until the early 1950s that the British inventor Sir Christopher Cockerell managed to produce a reliable working prototype. Believing that the military would be interested in such a machine he arranged demonstrations in Whitehall but was disappointed at the response, famously commenting that 'the Navy said it was a plane, not a boat; the Royal Air Force said it was a boat, not a plane; and the Army were plain not interested'. This lack of official enthusiasm saw the device removed from the 'secret list' and developed for commercial purposes. However, Cockerell maintained his belief that the hovercraft, with its extraordinary ability to cross both solid terrain – almost regardless of condition and topography – and water, might have military applications.

Vickers had supplied the first commercial hovercraft in the summer of 1962, but a month or so earlier had announced a hybrid Land Rover hovercraft that was quickly dubbed the Hover Rover. The device consisted of a 109in Series II with a second engine in the cargo bay driving a pair of vertically-mounted

lift fans. An inflatable rubber skirt was fitted around the perimeter of the vehicle but, unlike most hovercraft, the vehicle was still driven by its wheels, the hover fans being used to provide sufficient lift to prevent the weight of the machine from bogging it down in soft and marshy ground; for normal road use the skirt was lifted. The vehicle was trialled by FVRDE during 1962–63, but there were no purchases.

A second such vehicle that more closely resembled a conventional hovercraft was also constructed, being powered by a single large lift fan mounted horizontally. Again, it was certainly tested by the military authorities but never entered service.

## Amphibious 'lightweight'

In the late 1960s FVRDE trialled an amphibious 'lightweight' that had been constructed by adding flotation units to one of the early pre-production vehicles.

Heavily modified to suit its proposed amphibious role, the vehicle featured a large flotation unit – looking rather like glass-fibre-covered foam plastic – fitted to the rear. Similar units were attached to either side of the vehicle, mounted on outriggers, and at the front, where the headlamps were relocated. It is not clear whether or not the flotation units were removable. Propulsion in the water was achieved via a single Dowty hydrojet unit fitted centrally at the rear, driven via a power take-off. Clearly the engine would need to have been waterproofed, and there was an exhaust pipe extension attached to

**RIGHT The Vickers 'Hover Rover' consisted of a 109in Series II with a second engine in the cargo bay driving a pair of vertically-mounted lift fans; an inflatable rubber skirt was fitted around the perimeter allowing the weight of the vehicle to be spread over a large footprint. Although there were FVRDE trials during 1962–63, there were no purchases.**
*(Tank Museum)*

**ABOVE AND RIGHT** In the late 1960s one of the early pre-production 'lightweights' was fitted with flotation units to provide an amphibious capability. Propulsion in the water was achieved via a single Dowty hydrojet unit fitted centrally at the rear, driven by a power take-off. *(Tank Museum)*

the left-hand side of the windscreen, with an air-intake snorkel in the same position on the driver's side. A non-standard canvas top was fitted, with the frame lacking the rearmost support.

Trials were carried out on Horsea Lake near Portsmouth. Performance in the water was good. Nothing further seems to have come of the idea, but the FVRDE records indicate that the prototype was transferred to the Amphibious Trials & Development Unit (ATDU) at Instow before being sold in 1971. At one time it was part of the Dunsfold Collection.

**RIGHT** The amphibious 'lightweight' was trialled at Horsea Lake, near Portsmouth, and performance in the water was said to be good... although the vehicle has clearly stalled in this photograph. It is not clear whether or not the flotation units were removable, but the extended width of the vehicle must have made normal driving difficult. *(Tank Museum)*

'The Land Rover 110 Heavy Duty 6x6 is now
in volume production for the Australian Army
after several years development trialling against
international competition.'

**Land Rover Australia Limited sales leaflet**
November 1989

## Chapter Seven

# Licence-built military Land Rovers

Such was the demand for the Land Rover following its 1948 launch that the vehicles were ultimately licence-built for both military and civilian service in Australia by JRA, in Belgium by Minerva, in Turkey by Otokar, in West Germany by Tempo, and under the name Santana in Spain. Land Rovers were also assembled from CKD kits in Brazil, Kenya, Malaysia, Morocco, New Zealand, Nigeria, Trinidad, Spain, Zaire, Zambia and Zimbabwe.

**OPPOSITE** Dating back to 1982, the Australian 'Perentie' project saw the Australian Defence Force procure 2,500 1-ton 4x4 utility vehicles, and 400 6x6 machines rated at 2 tons, some of which were equipped as ambulances.
*(Australian Department of Defence)*

# Minerva

In 1899 Dutchman Sylvain de Jong established the Minerva car company, exhibiting a prototype *voiturette* and a light van at the Antwerp Cycle Show before launching a Panhard-style motorcar in 1902. In 1922 de Jong's company acquired a factory in the Mortsel suburb of Antwerp, and in 1924 started producing commercial vehicles. Financial difficulties led to Minerva being taken over by Mathieu Van Roggen's Impéria company in 1935.

Minerva resumed production of commercial vehicles after the end of World War Two, but financial difficulties meant that the company was unable to develop a new motorcar. A possible lifeline appeared at the end of the 1940s when the Belgian Army indicated that it was searching for a replacement for its stocks of ageing American Jeeps. Although Minerva was not in a position to design and build a military utility vehicle from scratch, Van Roggen was keen to secure the work to help fill the under-utilised Mortsel factory, and in early 1951 was granted a licence to build Land Rovers in Belgium. A contract to supply the Belgian Army with an initial quantity of 2,500 locally-built Land Rovers followed.

Designated the Minerva TT (*tout terrain*), the vehicle was effectively an 80in Series I, constructed using CKD kits supplied from Solihull. These CKD kits included the chassis, the Rover 1,997cc F-head engine, axles, four-speed gearbox and transfer case, and the bulkhead pressing. Some 63 per cent of the content of the vehicle, including the body, lighting equipment, top, tyres, body fittings, fuel tanks and upholstery, was of local origin, and later production may have used a boxed-in frame manufactured in Belgium, identifiable by the lack of the power take-off hole in the rear cross-member. The locally-produced body differed in various details from the standard Solihull product, most notably by being constructed from steel, which brought a weight penalty of more than 150lb (68kg). More obvious were the slope-faced front mudguards that were produced using simple press tools. The radiator grille was also different, consisting of a framed grille with separate pressed-steel slotted panels fitted to either side under the headlamps. A large cast aluminium badge was fitted at the top of the grille, showing the helmeted head of the Roman goddess Minerva, with the legend 'Licence Rover' or the familiar Land Rover oval underneath.

At the rear the hinged tailgate was replaced by a fixed panel carrying a jerrycan holder, and sometimes a spare wheel. Inside, the driver and front-seat passenger were provided with a pair of square-backed seats separated by a tool locker, and there was an additional inward-facing seat in the rear, on the right-hand side. Weather equipment consisted of a one-piece top and rear enclosure that included a roll-up rear panel glazed with two small transparent lights.

Production started on 12 September 1951, and the capacity of the production line was said to be 50 vehicles a day: 1,895 examples had been constructed by July 1952. In 1954 the 80in chassis was replaced by the 86in, but later that year the licence agreement was cancelled following disputes between the two companies. Production continued until 30 October 1956, with a further 900 CKD kits being supplied as part of a settlement agreement between Rover and Minerva. Total military production was 5,921 vehicles, of which 8,805 were of the 80in wheelbase.

Alongside the standard open-backed cargo/utility vehicle, other variants included a 24V FFR (fitted for radio) vehicle with a screened electrical system; a two-stretcher

**BELOW** Built in Mortsel, Belgium, between 1951 and 1956, the Minerva TT (*tout terrain*) was based on the 80in Series I, and constructed using CKD kits supplied from Solihull. The locally-produced body differed in many ways from the original and was constructed from steel. (Simon Thomson)

field ambulance with extending stretcher gear and a hood extension at the rear; and a dual-control driver-training vehicle. A small number of Minervas were later converted for the parachute/commando role, with strengthened suspension, outboard headlamps, an armoured shuttered grille, blackout lights, front-mounted spare wheel, armoured-glass screens and a rear stowage basket; armaments included three FN MAG 7.62mm machine guns. Airfield-defence vehicles were also produced, carrying 0.30in or 7.62mm machine guns, and as late as 1980 13 vehicles were modified to carry the MILAN infantry light anti-tank missile.

From October 1953 a version of the Minerva TT had also been marketed to civilian customers, both as an open cargo vehicle and as a short-wheelbase station wagon, and by 1955–56 Minerva had designed and produced their own all-terrain vehicles. The Continental-engined TT-C20 (80in) and TT-C22 (86in) models were intended for the civilian market, whilst the TT-M20 (80in) was for the military, but the vehicles were commercially unsuccessful and Minerva went into liquidation in 1958.

## Tempo-Land Rover

In early 1952 the German Federal Border Guards (*Bundesgrenzschutz*, or BGS) sought tenders from a number of manufacturers for a six-seater cross-country vehicle to be used for patrolling the border with East Germany. Domestic manufacturers showed little interest, but in the spring of that same year the BGS conducted trials directly comparing the home-grown Unimog 410 against the 80in Series I. Although the Land Rover apparently emerged as the better vehicle for the job, the BGS was keen to purchase home-grown products and, anyway, the Rover factory was not in a position

**RIGHT A number of Minervas were adapted for the parachute/commando role, and were fitted with heavy-duty suspension, armoured-glass screens, an armoured shuttered grille, outboard headlamps, blackout lights, front-mounted spare wheel and a rear stowage basket. Standard armaments included three 7.62mm machine guns.** *(Simon Thomson)*

**ABOVE A Land Rover, but not as we know it! The distinctive front mudguards of the Minerva TT were designed to be constructed using very simple press tools.** *(Warehouse Collection)*

**LEFT Standard Minerva TT utility vehicle.** *(Warehouse Collection)*

to supply the required number of vehicles against the required timescale.

One of the German companies that had shown an interest in securing the contract was Vidal & Sohn, owners of Tempo-Werke in Hamburg-Harburg, and in late 1952 Oscar Vidal approached Land Rover seeking a licence to assemble Land Rovers in Germany using body and other parts of local origin. The licence was granted in January 1953, and between April and August of that year somewhere between 100 and 189 vehicles were assembled by Tempo-Werke using chassis bulkheads, axles, gearboxes and power units supplied from Solihull. The engine cover and grille were also supplied from Britain, but the remainder of the body – which was generally of steel construction – was produced locally by Herbert Vidal & Company, which was owned by Oscar Vidal's brother.

There were considerable differences when compared to the Solihull product, most noticeably the high-sided rear body, centrally positioned spare-wheel carrier and full-length

doors. A locker was built into the front/top of each front mudguard, and the canvas top was designed to fold rather than be removed; a stowage box fitted across the engine cover was designed to hold the side-screens when these were not in place. Flashing direction indicators were mounted on the sides of the front mudguards, with a flashing blue light and siren on the right-hand mudguard or ahead of the radiator. Some examples were also fitted with a front-mounted mechanically driven capstan winch, and there was a full-width bumper at the rear. Inside the body, the centre seat was omitted and there were two tip-up seats at the front, with provision for four men on inward-facing lateral benches in the rear. If a radio was carried it was mounted between the front seats, and a heater was fitted as standard equipment.

Power came from the standard 1,997cc four-cylinder petrol engine, driving through a Rover four-speed gearbox and two-speed transfer box. A high-capacity Bosch generator was fitted, and the electrical system was wired on a negative earth return rather than the positive return of Solihull-produced vehicles of the period.

In 1954 the wheelbase was increased to 86in and a number of other changes were made. For example, the spare wheel was moved to the normal position on the engine cover, meaning that the stowage box for the side windows was deleted. The mudguard lockers remained, and stowage clips were also provided on the engine cover and the tops of the mudguards for pioneer tools; width indicators were also fitted. Cable trunking was fitted across the width of the body behind the front seats, and there were twin fuel tanks, together with an auxiliary tank under the passenger seat; this doubled the original 11-gallon (50-litre) capacity. A jerrycan was carried at the rear. Somewhere between 80 and 150 examples were produced in this form.

In 1956 100 of the best BGS Tempo-Land Rovers were allocated to the newly-formed *Bundeswehr*, and the vehicles remained in service until the mid-1960s. Keen to obtain further orders, in 1959 Vidal & Sohn produced two Series II-based vehicles as demonstrators. However, all future *Bundeswehr* Land Rovers were supplied directly from Britain.

# Santana

Established by the Spanish Government as Metalurgica de Santa Ana SA in February 1955, the Linares-based Santana Company was originally formed to build combine harvesters and other agricultural machinery. However, in 1956 Santana negotiated a licence with Rover to produce Land Rovers in Spain; in return Rover acquired 49 per cent of the company shares. The first Spanish-built Land Rovers were Series IIs, which went on sale in 1959 with a choice of 2.25-litre petrol engine or 2-litre diesel. The vehicles were produced from CKD kits supplied from Solihull. For the first 1,500 units the local content was 75 per cent, but this had risen to 95 per cent by the time 2,500 vehicles had been completed. By 1980 Santana was producing 18,000 vehicles a year and the company had become a significant supplier to South America, North Africa and other Spanish-speaking areas.

At first the Spanish Army purchased standard civilian-style vehicles, but two special military models appeared in the early 1970s. The first was the Model 88 *Militar* 'lightweight'; the other, a similar 109in vehicle rated at 1 ton, was described as the Model 109 *Militar*. Alongside these machines, Santana also continued to produce civilian Land Rovers, including the forward-control 1300 – which was also bodied as a military ambulance – and Series II and III cargo and station wagon models. Santana was the first builder of Land Rovers to use a turbocharged diesel engine, offering a 2,286cc four-cylinder unit in the 'Super T' models as early as 1983.

By 1990 Santana had produced 300,000 vehicles. Rover then disposed all financial interest in the company, terminating the manufacturing licence agreement at the same time. The company subsequently entered into an agreement with Suzuki and continued to manufacture off-road vehicles until late 2011, when it was closed down.

## Model 88 *Militar*

Based on the 88in Series IIA, and rated at ½ ton, the Model 88 *Militar* adopted a similar design approach to the British 'lightweight', with a simple body designed to reduce the total weight to allow air-portability; unlike the British 'lightweight', the body panels of the Model 88 did not need to be demounted. Development started in 1969, and the Model 88 was adopted as the standard vehicle in its class by the Spanish Army. The first of 3,500 were delivered in 1970, and production ceased in 1990.

Power was provided by a locally-built version of the Rover 2,286cc four-cylinder petrol engine producing 70bhp, and driving through a four-speed gearbox and two-speed transfer case. A 2,286cc 62bhp diesel engine option was also available. Distinctive features of the Model 88 included high cutaway angular wheel arches, small recessed headlights (moved into the front mudguard faces in 1972), double bumpers and a radiator grille that was flush with the faces of the front mudguards.

Both soft-top and fully-enclosed versions were produced, the latter using a glass-fibre composite hardtop. In its standard form the Model 88 provided seating for two men in the cab, and either four men, on inward-facing seats, or half a ton of cargo in the rear compartment. The vehicle could also be coupled to a 1-ton light gun or cargo trailer. Other variants included a hardtop command or communications version, equipped with a 42Ah or 90Ah 24V alternator, and weapons carriers mounting either the MILAN anti-tank missile, M40 106mm anti-tank recoilless rifle, 60mm mortar, or 7.62mm or 0.50in machine guns. There was also a deep-wading version designed for the Spanish Marines, capable of immersion in water up to 74in (1,880mm).

**ABOVE The Spanish company Santana was originally established to build agricultural implements, but in 1956 started to produce Land Rovers under licence. The strictly military but rather ungainly Model 88 was a lightweight machine intended for air-portability, and was introduced in the early 1970s.** *(Warehouse Collection)*

**RIGHT** Photographed in the United Arab Emirates in 2011, this 1975 Santana Model 88 is equipped with the M40A1 106mm recoilless rifle. The vehicle served with the Abu Dhabi Defence Force (ADDF) between 1975 and 1983.
*(Simon Thomson)*

**RIGHT** Sharing its eccentric looks with the Model 88 was the long-wheelbase 1-ton Santana Model 109.
*(Warehouse Collection)*

**BELOW** When photographed, this Santana Model 109 general-service vehicle was in the care of the Dunsfold Collection.
*(Warehouse Collection)*

Constructed on a galvanised chassis to resist corrosion, the vehicle was equipped with a snorkel, waterproofed ancillaries and a depressurised breathing system for the engine.

The Model 88 was also offered on the civilian market, where it was named *Ligero*, and an unlicensed version was built in Iran in the 1980s by Morrattab, using CKD kits supplied by Santana.

## Model 109 *Militar*

Based on the long-wheelbase Series IIA, and then on the Series III, the Model 109 *Militar* was effectively a 1-ton variant of the Model 88. It entered production in 1973 and was produced in both military and civilian versions, with examples supplied to the Spanish, Egyptian and Moroccan Armies. By the time production ended in 1990 the total number built had reached 2,000.

Like the smaller Model 88, there was a choice of 2,286cc four-cylinder diesel or petrol engines, as well as a locally-produced 3,429cc six-cylinder petrol or diesel unit. All versions shared the same type of four-speed gearbox and two-speed transfer case. Twin fuel tanks were fitted with a total capacity of 25 gallons (115 litres), giving a greatly increased range of operation.

The standard military variant was an eight- to ten-seater troop or cargo carrier, equipped with either a hardtop or soft-top; this version was also suitable as a weapons mount. Other variants included a hardtop communications vehicle, equipped with a 50Ah or 90Ah 24V alternator, screened electrical equipment and oil cooler, and available to suit various different radio configurations; a light recovery vehicle with a folding 1-ton electrically-operated jib in the cargo area; and a fully-enclosed four-stretcher ambulance. There was also a snorkel-equipped deep-wading version available, examples of which were used by the Spanish Marines.

ABOVE Rated at 2 tons, the civilian forward-control Santana S-2000 was also adapted for a number of military roles. This flat-bed variant is carrying a US-style S250 aluminium shelter. *(Warehouse Collection)*

ABOVE Australian-built Series II/IIA showing the large brush guard (or 'roo bar in Australian parlance), distinctive cutaway mudguards and lack of sills. *(Phil Royal)*

## Santana S-2000 *Militar*

In 1981 Santana introduced a 2-ton forward-control vehicle with a 101in wheelbase. Known as the S-2000, it was produced in both civilian and military versions, and examples were purchased by the Spanish Army and the armed forces of several other nations.

The S-2000 *Militar* was powered by a six-cylinder 3,429cc petrol or diesel engine, driving through a four-speed manual gearbox and two-speed transfer case. It was equipped with a distinctive flat-panelled body that could be used as a 12-man personnel carrier, and other variants included a cargo vehicle, generator truck, tanker, command post, mobile workshop, container vehicle, and a mount for a 20mm Oerlikon anti-aircraft cannon. A chassis-cab version was also available for specialised bodywork.

# JRA Perentie

Since the early 1960s the Australian Defence Force (ADF) had favoured locally-produced Series II and IIA Land Rovers as the standard military utility vehicle, before moving on to the Series III and the Defender. Local modifications included additional stowage facilities, increased ride height, oversized cutaway front mudguards, protected taillights, and distinctive heavy-duty bush guards at the front. Alongside the cargo variants there were also ambulance, fire-fighting and workshop vehicles. Many of these vehicles are now being superseded by more modern machinery, and in late 2011 it was announced

that the ADF would be disposing of some 3,000 older Land Rovers through the Defence Disposals Agency – many of them examples of the uniquely Australian 'Project Perentie' vehicles.

In July 1982, under the code name 'Project Perentie', the ADF announced that it was to procure 2,500 1-ton and 400 2-ton utility vehicles to replace a handful of ageing Series II and IIA Land Rovers fitted with specialised bodies, plus a larger number of Series III vehicles. Seven companies indicated an interest in the project, including Jaguar-Rover Australia (JRA). Of these seven, just two – JRA and Mercedes-Benz Unimog – were asked to provide vehicles for trials. Both of JRA's submissions were based on the Defender 110, but with power coming from an Isuzu 4BD1 four-cylinder diesel engine, the engine of the

BELOW Stripped of its doors, top and supporting frame, and with the windscreen folded forwards, this Australian Series II/IIA makes an excellent long-range patrol vehicle. *(Phil Royal)*

2-ton 6x6 variant being turbocharged. In both cases the engine was coupled to the four-speed transmission of the early Range Rover.

The 2-ton 6x6 variant, which was developed especially for this project, borrowed some design principles from a Sandringham Stage One 6x6 development vehicle that had been supplied to JRA by SMC Engineering of Bristol for possible civilian use in 1981. However, the Sandringham chassis was rejected as unsuitable, and a new, purpose-designed heavy-duty galvanised-steel frame was designed, with a fabricated rear section of rectangular tube to support the rear bogie. The front and rear axles were wider than standard, and were fitted with lower ratio gears to accommodate the increased weight, while drive to the rearmost axle was by a separate propeller shaft from the transfer box power take-off.

Eight evaluation vehicles were constructed, four of each type – three of these were submitted for assessment by the Trials and Proving Wing at Monegeeta, near Melbourne, with the fourth retained by JRA for in-house assessment. Following completion of the trials at Monegeeta the vehicles were submitted for a user assessment phase, which included hot/wet trials

at Tully in North Queensland, and cold weather trials at Khancoban in the Snowy Mountains. At the end of the trials the two manufacturers were invited to tender for production. The contract stated that the vehicles were to be produced over a three- to four-year period commencing in May 1986 and to continue until 1990: volume production of the 1-ton vehicle was scheduled to begin in May 1987, and for the 2-ton variant in March 1989. When the tendering process closed

**ABOVE** Satellite terminal assemblage unit mounted on the back of a Perentie 6x6. The equipment is sited at the main sports oval at HMAS *Stirling*, Garden Island, Western Australia, and is being used to provide communications coverage in order to maintain a secure domestic air environment. *(Australian Department of Defence)*

**ABOVE RIGHT** Flying Officer Alex Barbaro marches through the pouring rain alongside a Perentie 6x6 'Parakeet' satellite communications vehicle as it crawls across the terrain to a new tactical air command post (TACP). *(Australian Department of Defence)*

in October 1983 it was announced that the contract would be awarded to JRA.

The 1-ton variant was designated as the 'Land Rover 110 4x4', but is generally identified as the MC2 4x4 'Perentie'. Six basic types were produced, including soft-top cargo vehicle, hardtop and soft-top communications vehicles, command post, commander's vehicle, personnel carrier/station wagon, and an uprated 1.2-ton surveillance vehicle. The larger vehicle, which was now fitted with a wider, three-man cab, was known as the 'Land Rover 110 6x6', or MC2HD 6x6 'Perentie', and was produced in three variants: cargo truck, artillery vehicle and ambulance. Both 4x4 and 6x6 versions were also used as the basis of a long-range patrol vehicle for the Australian SAS; the smaller 4x4 version resembled the British SAS desert patrol vehicle (DPV), whilst the extra length of the 6x6 provided considerably enhanced carrying capacity.

Between 1994 and 1998 additional vehicles were built for the ADF under the code name 'Project Bushranger', and large numbers of the 'Perentie' vehicles were also given a midlife rebuild in 2006 to extend their service life. Once production was under way the 2-ton 6x6 vehicle was also offered worldwide, with the option of a 3.5-litre V8 petrol engine. There wasn't much interest outside of Australia, but a further ten examples, fitted with a removable 'logistics' body, were constructed for Oman.

**ABOVE** Students of Tactical Communications (TACTCOMMS) course 0039 swarm over and around a Perentie 6x6 'Parakeet' satellite communications vehicle in an effort to transform it into a TACP as quickly as possible. *(Australian Department of Defence)*

**LEFT** The Omani government purchased 10 Perentie 6x6 trucks fitted with what was described as a removable 'logistics body'. *(Warehouse Collection)*

## Otokar

The Istanbul-based Otokar company was established in 1963, initially producing Magirus-Deutz buses under licence. During the 1970s it was purchased by the Koc Group and, in mid-1978 started to produce armoured security vehicles. Within a decade Koc had negotiated a licence agreement to produce Land Rover Defenders in Turkey, initially for the

RIGHT Otokar Defender 110 station wagon. *(Koc Group)*

RIGHT Otokar Defender 110-based battlefield ambulance. *(Koc Group)*

Turkish armed forces but subsequently for the civilian market too.

The Turkish-built Defender is manufactured at the company's Sakarya plant, with both military and civilian versions produced in all three standard wheelbase lengths – 90in, 110in, and 127/130in. Standard body styles include station wagon, hardtop, and single- or double-cab pickup. Specialised military variants include field ambulance, command vehicle, troop carrier, search and rescue vehicle, field workshop vehicle and weapons platform. The Turkish Defenders are currently powered by the 2.5-litre 300Tdi turbocharged four-cylinder diesel engine, in combination with a five-speed manual gearbox and two-speed transfer case with locking differential. Otokar also produces a discreetly-armoured personnel carrier intended as transport for military and high-ranking civilian personnel. Based on the Defender 110 drivetrain and engine, the vehicle has the appearance of a standard Land Rover station wagon but is fitted with a body that has been armoured to 'military standards'.

Additionally, the company has a range of 4x4 light armoured tactical wheeled vehicles, developed using technologies licensed from Land Rover and American company AM General.

### Armoured patrol vehicle

The Otokar armoured patrol vehicle (APV) is a lightly-armoured personnel carrier (APC) for military and internal security roles. Sharing 80 per cent of its mechanical components with the Defender 110, including the 300Tdi four-cylinder turbocharged diesel engine, five-speed manual gearbox, axles and suspension, the APV can also be adapted for use as an ambulance, airfield security vehicle, workshop or repair vehicle, and command vehicle, and for the police and internal security roles. It is also marketed as the Defender 110 APC.

The standard welded steel hull is designed to accommodate six fully-equipped personnel seated on inward-facing bench seats, together with two men in the cab, and provides protection from 7.62mm NATO ball ammunition fired at point-blank range. Machine-pressed glass-fibre composite armour plates are fitted under the floor to deflect blast from anti-personnel mines, grenades and improvised explosive devices, and the driver has a two-piece multi-layer laminated windscreen, with small windows set into the door tops. All of the windows are protected to the same ballistic standards as the hull and include anti-spall polycarbonate liners. Side and rear vision and firing ports are inserted into the hull, and a roof hatch or a simple open turret can be fitted, typically mounting a 7.62mm or 0.50in machine gun. Air-conditioning and internal ventilation facilities are provided as standard, as are run-flat tyres mounted on three-piece heavy steel wheels. Optional equipment includes a barricade remover, public address system, searchlights, electrically-operated winch, etc.

## Akrep attack/defence vehicle

Introduced in the early-1990s, the Otokar *Akrep* ('Scorpion') is a light armoured reconnaissance vehicle intended for escort, reconnaissance and border-control duties. Sharing some 70 per cent of its mechanical components with the Defender 110, including the 300Tdi turbocharged diesel engine, five-speed transmission, axles and suspension, it is constructed around an angular armoured-steel box hull of high-hardness steel that provides protection from 7.62mm NATO ball ammunition fired at point-blank range; small vision ports are provided in the rear body and in the rear door, along with firing ports. Access is provided via forward doors for the driver and front passenger, and a single, side-hung door at the rear, and all of the glazed areas are of multi-layer laminated glass, with anti-spall polycarbonate liners. The front-mounted engine has full armoured protection.

Air-conditioning equipment, heater and demister, run-flat tyres, infrared and black-out driving lamps, and antenna mount are provided as standard, and an electrical winch, smoke grenade dischargers, communications equipment and satnav system are also available at extra cost.

Standard variants include an armoured personnel carrier, mobile ground surveillance vehicle, internal security vehicle and weapons platform, the last equipped with either a single 7.62mm GPMG in an overhead mount, turret-mounted 12.7mm machine gun, or a remote-controlled roof turret mounting a pair of 7.62mm GPMGs with a forward-looking infrared vision system to allow observation and target acquisition.

**ABOVE** Sharing 80 per cent of its mechanical components with the Defender 110, including the engine and transmission, the Otokar APV is also marketed by Land Rover as the Defender APC. *(Koc Group)*

**BELOW** The Otokar *Akrep* is a light armoured reconnaissance vehicle intended for escort, reconnaissance and border-control duties, and shares around 70 per cent of its mechanical components with the Defender 110, including the engine, transmission, axles and suspension. Standard variants include an armoured personnel carrier, mobile ground surveillance vehicle, internal security vehicle and weapons platform. *(Koc Group)*

'The TUL/TUM is the "workhorse" of the Army's operational B vehicle fleet, fulfilling a range of roles from administrative vehicle to command vehicle and weapons carrier. It represents the largest single range of types in military service.'
**Official Ministry of Defence publication**
1993

## Chapter Eight

# The soldier's view

Serving soldiers, at least in the British Army, are rarely sentimental about the kit that they use. Whilst they may be quick to criticise something that is clearly not up to the job, genuine fitness for purpose might receive little more than grudging admiration, and the Land Rover is something of an unsung hero. However, it is clearly testament to the essential suitability of the vehicle for its myriad roles that it has already clocked-up almost 65 years of military service.

**OPPOSITE** Another typical day in the War Against Terror. The lead vehicle is a **WMIK-equipped Defender RDV** mounting a 7.62mm GPMG; the second vehicle is equipped with a **MILAN** anti-tank missile launcher. *(MoD)*

The Land Rover was originally created as a dual-purpose agricultural utility vehicle, designed to perform the functions for which Rover's Maurice Wilks had found the American Jeep so useful. Having created what might be described as a British Jeep, it should be no surprise that the Land Rover also found favour with the military. Slightly curious – particularly bearing in mind the level of enthusiasm for the Land Rover in 'civvy street' – is the apparent indifference of the average squaddie to Solihull's finest. During World War Two, Jeeps were frequently given pet names, and their off-road capabilities were spoken of in almost hushed and reverent tones. Having looked at what must be thousands of military Land Rover photographs, none appears to show a Land Rover with a pet name – and the attitude of the average serving soldier to the vehicle seems to indicate that it is simply a tool to do a job.

Maybe it is a classic case of familiarity breeding contempt?

## British Army service

The Land Rover started to enter military service in Britain in 1949. It was originally a short-term measure to supplement the ageing World War Two Jeeps whilst development of the Austin Champ was completed. Between

**RIGHT** Pristine 86in Series I GS cargo vehicle photographed in Malaya in the mid-1950s. *(Warehouse Collection)*

**BELOW** Line-up of 86in Series Is 'somewhere in the Middle East'. *(IWM, GOV10683)*

**RIGHT** 88in Series I equipped as a communications vehicle. Land Rovers did not normally carry pioneer tools, but note the handy shovel stowed in the rear bumperette should the vehicle become bogged down. *(IWM, GOV10676)*

**CENTRE** Off-road ability is probably not significant for a mobile recruiting office and this 88in Series I station wagon is one of the rare 4x2 vehicles acquired in the late-1950s. Described as a 'utility car', the transfer box was locked in the 'high' range and the front axle was a simple tubular design to which the standard swivel housings were attached. *(Warehouse Collection)*

**BELOW** An ageing long-wheelbase Series III heading up a couple of Defender 110s pulls up at a checkpoint in Croatia. The vehicles are assigned to IFOR, the NATO-led multi-national peacekeeping force in Bosnia and Herzegovina during 1995–96, and are participating in 'Operation Joint Endeavour'. *(US DoD, Sergeant Brian Gavin)*

1949 and 1952 the Jeep and the Land Rover served together until deliveries of the Champ commenced. From 1952 examples of all three vehicles served together until the last British Army Jeeps were discharged in about 1956–57. A year later the War Office went on record stating that the Land Rover was the British Army's standard utility vehicle, and by 1966 the Champs had all gone too.

Despite having to fight off a challenge from the upstart Austin Gipsy and the Stonefield during the 1960s and 1970s, the Land Rover

**ABOVE** A Westland Lynx battlefield helicopter makes a rendezvous with British troops in a WMIK-equipped Defender RDV. The Lynx AH.7 attack/utility helicopter forms a vital component of the British Commando Helicopter Force (CHF). *(MoD)*

**LEFT** British troops with the much-criticised Snatch Defender. *(MoD)*

had the field to itself until the Pinzgauer 710 started to enter service in the mid-1990s. Nevertheless, the Land Rover remains the most numerous utility vehicle in British Army service.

Although most Land Rovers will have spent most of their lives on nothing more exciting than the transportation of personnel and cargo safely behind the lines, the vehicle saw its first real action in Korea in 1950, where it proved itself to be more than capable of doing anything that the Jeep could do. It might have been a different story when the Champs appeared in 1952, but by that time the fighting was almost over. Since that time Land Rovers have almost certainly participated in every conflict in which the British Army has been involved, as well as going wherever the British Army was based

or trained, including Aden, Canada, Gibraltar, Hong Kong, Norway and West Germany.

During the mid-1950s there were Land Rovers in Malaya during the Communist insurgency, in Cyprus following the Greek-Cypriot EOKA campaign for independence, and in Kenya during the Mau Mau uprisings. Both Land Rovers and Champs were despatched to Egypt in 1956 during the ill-fated Anglo-French attempt to wrest control of the Suez Canal back from the nationalist government of Colonel Gamal Abdul Nasser. The SAS took their iconic SIIA 'Pink Panthers' to southern Oman in 1968–69, when they were busy fighting the Dhofar rebels. In Northern Ireland, the distinctive VPK Makrolon-armoured Land Rovers (dubbed 'piglets') became a familiar sight on the streets of Belfast and Derry/Londonderry during 'the troubles' that were sparked off in 1969 – as did the more-heavily armoured Shorlands and other Land Rover-derived patrol vehicles of the Royal Ulster Constabulary; and it was also in Northern Ireland that the composite armoured Snatch Land Rovers made their first appearance.

Immediately prior to the Falklands conflict in 1982 Rover received an emergency order for some 600 Series III vehicles manufactured to what was described as a simplified 'CL' (commercial) specification – or perhaps they were nothing more than civilian vehicles diverted from domestic sales. However, they were unfortunately loaded onto the *Atlantic Conveyor*, which was struck by an Argentine Exocet missile, and ended up at the bottom of

the Atlantic. Aside from a small number of '101' gun tractors, and perhaps a couple of FFW communications vehicles, few military Land Rovers were available on the islands during the campaign.

White-painted British Army Land Rovers have also helped carry out peace-keeping missions on behalf of the United Nations in Bosnia, Cyprus, Kosovo and elsewhere. And, more recently, Land Rovers have seen action in Afghanistan, Iraq and Kuwait, where the Snatch armoured vehicles have come in for heavy criticism for failing to protect crews adequately against improvised explosive devices.

Sometimes the Land Rovers have been more directly involved in combat than was normal. For example, during the 'Operation Buffalo' nuclear tests held at Maralinga in South Australia in September–October 1956 half a dozen seemingly brand-new Series I Land Rovers were exposed directly to the effects of nuclear blast alongside a clutch of Daimler Dingos and three Centurion Mk 3 tanks. Whilst the Centurions remained largely driveable after the event, the Land Rovers escaped from the blast rather less well!

The recent trend towards what is being called 'asymmetric warfare', with heavy reliance on IEDs as a means of harrying and discomforting a better-equipped foe, has seen the Land Rover largely relegated to behind-the-lines roles. Nevertheless, thousands remain in service and the military Land Rover remains a familiar sight on Britain's roads.

**LEFT** Launching an unmanned Desert Hawk 'drone' aircraft from a WMIK-equipped Defender RDV. *(MoD)*

**BELOW** Wolf Defender with wire-mesh protection for the windscreen leading a convoy of GKN Saxon armoured personnel carriers through the streets of a Middle East town. *(MoD)*

**ABOVE** Royal Marines' short-wheelbase Wolf TUL showing off its wading capabilities. *(Warehouse Collection)*

**RIGHT** Pulse ambulance in Helmand Province, forming part of a medical emergency response team. *(MoD, Dave Husbands)*

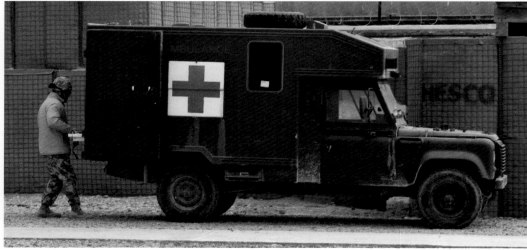

# Service overseas

**U**nlike many specialised military vehicles Land Rovers remain relatively affordable, and when this is combined with the vehicle's legendary versatility and reliability it should be no surprise that the Land Rover is probably the most widely-exported military vehicle in the world.

The first enquiry for military Land Rovers came from India, and although this was not followed by any orders, by 1963 Rover was able to claim that there were Land Rovers in service with 26 armed services across the world. Indeed, by the 1970s it seems that there were few armies outside the Soviet Bloc, plus any number of paramilitary organisations – including the United Nations and various aid agencies – that had not at one time or another operated military Land Rovers.

A full list of those operating military Land Rovers is an impressive roll call of nations. It includes Algeria, Angola, Australia, Belgium, Brazil, Brunei, Burma, Cambodia, Ceylon, Chile, Congo, Croatia, Cuba, Denmark, Egypt, Gambia, Ghana, Greece, Guyana, Hong Kong, Indonesia, Iran, Iraq, Ireland, Italy, Jamaica, Jordan, Kenya, Kuwait, Lebanon, Libya, Malaysia, Morocco, Muscat, the Netherlands, New Zealand, Nicaragua, Nigeria, Oman, Peru, Portugal, Qatar, (the former) Rhodesia, Saudi Arabia, Sierra Leone, South Africa, Spain, Sudan, Switzerland, Syria, Tanzania, Thailand, Trinidad, Tunisia, Turkey, Uganda, Venezuela, West Germany, Zaire, Zambia, Zimbabwe... and even the United States of America.

**ABOVE Snatch armoured Defender in the distinctive white livery of the United Nations.** *(Land Rover Limited)*

Military-style Land Rovers, often discreetly armoured, have also often been deployed by news and media companies, aid agencies and charities operating in 'hot-spots' across the globe.

**BELOW LEFT Shorland Mk 5 APC in service with CNN Cable News Network.** *(Tank Museum)*

**BELOW Lightly-armoured Defender personnel carrier, prepared by Foley Specialist Vehicles. This vehicle is typical of machines used by charity, media or non-governmental agency personnel in 'hot spots'.** *(Warehouse Collection)*

'Every time we sell a Land Rover,
business gets a little tougher.'

**Rover Company Limited press
advertisement**
1977

## Chapter Nine

# The civilian's view

Whilst many ex-military Land Rovers are purchased because they are cheap, with the owner caring little about the vehicle's previous history, the ex-military Land Rover is at the same time very popular amongst British collectors and re-enactors. OK, so the 'bog standard' quarter-ton cargo variant might lack the combat chic of the World War Two Jeep, but it also costs a fraction of the price and will almost certainly cost less to maintain.

**OPPOSITE Military vehicle shows provide the perfect opportunity for like-minded enthusiasts to get together and compare notes.** *(Phil Royal)*

**ABOVE** Military Land Rovers can be found for sale in a variety of conditions, ranging from what might be described as 'parts vehicles' to low-mileage specimens that appear to have lived a very pampered life. *(Ian Young)*

**BELOW** Beware of vehicles that have been partially stripped... if the Army needed to salvage used parts to keep other vehicles running, then it will almost certainly not be easy to find these very same parts on the collectors' market. *(Ian Young)*

# Buying a military Land Rover

Although the expression 'time spent in reconnaissance is seldom wasted' is generally attributed to the Duke of Wellington it is more likely that it was first said by the 4th-century Chinese warrior Sun Tzu. However, regardless of who originally made this observation it is excellent advice, and holds equally good when undertaking the purchase and restoration of a military Land Rover as it does for those bent on taking over the known world.

As regards *where* you buy, it comes down to personal preference. At one extreme Land Rovers can still be found in the backs of barns, albeit they will inevitably be rather more agricultural than military, whilst later models are still being sold by the British Army, often in very tired condition. If neither of these approaches appeals, there are plenty of dealers (see 'Useful contacts', page 168), as well as private sales advertised in the military vehicle and club magazines. Be slightly wary of buying from mainstream classic-car dealers or classic-car auctions where values tend to be overinflated and the vehicles often over-restored.

**LEFT** The Wolf remains a scarce commodity in private hands and any vehicle that is offered for sale by the military will inevitably require considerable work. These two examples appear to be saveable. *(Ian Young)*

**LEFT** That distinctive pink colour is enough to increase the heart rate of any military Land Rover enthusiast, but these days finding a 'Pink Panther' that is ripe for restoration is about as likely as finding a dental chart for a Rhode Island Red. *(Ian Young)*

When considering a possible purchase, you don't need to be an expert – you just need to know where to look and to keep your eyes open and your wits about you. From a mechanical point of view a basic military Land Rover is a simple, straightforward machine in which it is difficult to hide faults. Whilst there is some scope for concealing the inevitable rust in the bulkhead or chassis members, the lack of trim means that every part of the body is literally on show – you can see both sides of most panels, and what you see is generally what you get. And if the vehicle is incomplete or in poor condition, remember that most parts are still available, literally off the shelf.

**BELOW** Strictly 'breaking for parts'! *(Ian Young)*

# AGRICULTURAL VEHICLES

Office : AGRICULTURAL VEHICLES,
HARCOURT HILL,
OXFORD.
Tel. 42602.

Depot : STANTON HARCOURT ROAD,
EYNSHAM,
OXON.
Tel. Eynsham 559.

### LAND-ROVER G.P. VEHICLE

All vehicles are direct ex-Ministry and unregistered, having been checked throughout and overhauled by the M.O.S., since when they have not been re-issued. Many
are fitted with brand new reconditioned engine assemblies.

These vehicles are identical to the civilian version, but, being in genuine low-
mileage condition, bear no comparison to a civilian used vehicle of similar age, as
can be seen immediately on inspection.

A four-speed synchromesh gearbox operates through a high and low ratio
transfer case giving a range of eight forward speeds. Four wheel drive is optionally
engaged by a separate gear lever.

Provision is made for fitting of P.T.O. and/or Winch.

They are of standard wheelbase length and fitted with petrol engine.

Canvas tops are fitted, although from time to time hard top versions are
available.

Price : £225 – £250.

Also available : Series 86 Land-Rovers—a later version, having longer wheelbase and longer body.

Price : £245 – £285.

And Series 88 : Price : £285 – £310.

The price variation is accounted for mainly by tyre and general condition.

## What to pay

The days of being able to buy 'ex-Ministry' Land
Rovers for silly money are long gone. Back in
the 1960s companies such as RR Services
and Agricultural Vehicles in Oxfordshire were
offering low-mileage, recently overhauled military
Series Is at prices ranging from £225 to £310
depending on age, tyres and general condition.
In today's money £225 is equal to £3,500,
and whilst this would certainly not be sufficient
to buy a good Series I, neither would it be
enough for an average Defender in ex-Ministry
condition.

As regards the 'bread and butter' Land
Rovers, the Series I has become increasingly
collectable over the past few years with well-
restored examples now commanding prices
of around £10–15,000. The average figure for
a vehicle requiring little work would tend to be
less than £5,000 and 'basket cases' can still be
found for less than £1,000. One of the problems
facing the would-be buyer of a 'genuine' military
Series I is the difficulty of actually verifying that
the vehicle is what it purports to be. All military
vehicles will originally have been fitted with a
data plate on the bulkhead or the inner front
mudguard, giving details of the vehicle type and
the contract, chassis and vehicle numbers, but
this is frequently missing. Look for evidence of
its position, which will be marked by four small
holes. Other clues as to the military origins of
the vehicle include multiple coats of indifferently-
applied overall Deep Bronze Green or NATO
matt green paint, white markings alongside
the transmission and axle oil fillers to indicate
the required grade of lubricant (*eg* 'OEP 220');
some military Series Is were also fitted with
split-rim 'combat' wheels, and grab handles
at the rear corners. Genuine military Series Is
remain comparatively rare.

The Series II, IIA and III are still considered
less desirable by collectors and, unless
equipped for a unique or unusual role, prices
are currently topping out at around £4–5,000.
Although it is slightly easier to identify an
ex-military Series II, IIA or III, it should be
pointed out that not all were fitted, for example,
with military lighting equipment or double
bumpers. Much the same is true of the
Defender, with a well-restored or low-mileage
vehicle that has been in private hands for some

LEFT A genuine military Series I is a rare commodity and prices are rising. This very pretty 86in vehicle was supplied under a huge 1955 contract.
(Simon Thomson)

BELOW Many military vehicle collectors also like to acquire relevant items of equipment, including de-activated weapons, enabling the creation of a realistic diorama.
(Simon Thomson)

time maybe selling at around £5,000 or less, depending on age. The maximum price for a vehicle direct from MoD stock is currently around £7,500 or more.

The military specials, such as the forward-control '101' and the Series II/IIA 'lightweight', have never been particularly popular outside the military vehicle collectors' market. In the past the '101' was considered to make a good 'safari'-type vehicle, although these days its thirst makes it less appealing, and with both vehicles the high percentage of non-standard parts used in their construction is seen as a negative by 'civilians'. Nevertheless, you should still expect to pay up to around £3,000 for a good 'lightweight' and perhaps twice as much for a '101' – a '101' Vampire was recently advertised at more than £8,000.

The 'holy grail' of military Land Rovers is

RIGHT Unusual vehicles will always attract attention from other enthusiasts – wives and girlfriends are allowed to remain mystified. The vehicle is the Australian OTAL amphibian.
(Warehouse Collection)

almost certainly an original Series IIA 'Pink Panther', and if you can find one of these you will need to dig very deep into your pocket indeed. But try to make sure that it is actually a genuine 'Pinkie'... there are replicas out there. Running a close second would be a genuine ex-military Wolf, very few of which have been demobbed. Other specials such as the Shorland armoured car, any of the 'special operations vehicles', Centaur, Snatch Defender or TACR-1 or TAC-T fire-crash-rescue truck, will be similarly expensive.

All prices are quoted as at spring 2012. And remember, it always costs more to restore a vehicle properly than to purchase the fruits of someone else's labour.

## Parts availability

The fact that there is often little difference between an ex-military Land Rover and its civilian equivalent, particularly with the older 'Series' vehicles, means that the availability of parts for rebuilding and maintaining Land Rovers is generally excellent. Reproduction parts are also available for older vehicles, including whole chassis and body panels, and the difficulties only

**ABOVE** The inclusion of a well-dressed tailor's dummy or two can make all the difference to a vehicle display... even when the vehicle is the iconic 'Pink Panther'. *(Warehouse Collection)*

**RIGHT** Well-restored and comprehensively equipped Series I SAS vehicle seen at the annual War & Peace Show. The downside of owning such a vehicle is that it is hardly appropriate for an occasional trip to the bank or supermarket! *(Simon Thomson)*

start to arise with those items that are unique to the military vehicles or with unusual vehicles that were constructed in small numbers. The exact specification of early military Land Rovers varied from one contract to another, but at least some of the special military components – including items such as front and rear lights, ignition system, tow hitch, rifle clips, etc – were shared with other military vehicles of the period, making them that bit easier to track down. But access to a proper military parts list is a must and you will still need to be prepared to spend considerable time searching for elusive items.

On the downside, it is unfortunate that, in the past, the relatively low price of ex-military Land Rovers meant that many were purchased by owners with no interest in the vehicle's history. This often resulted in the removal of the uniquely military fittings and equipment, including 24V alternators, regulators and wiring, making these items difficult to track down.

The forward-control '101', the 'lightweight' and the Wolf Defender XD share far fewer components with the civilian vehicles, so finding parts for these will be a little more difficult. Curiously there are currently Wolf parts available on the surplus market, despite most of the

**TOP** The boxy body of the typical Land Rover ambulance makes an excellent basis for a camping conversion ... and there's even room for the dog! *(Warehouse Collection)*

**CENTRE** This prototype for the Rangers special operations vehicle is the only one of its kind in private hands in the UK. *(Simon Thomson)*

**LEFT** Acquiring a Scammell 8x6 DROPS vehicle might be a better approach than actually driving the vehicle from one event to another. *(Phil Royal)*

vehicles for which they were intended remaining in service. A problem has also recently arisen with Snatch vehicles that have come up for sale through the usual disposal channels: many of them are damaged or incomplete, and finding replacement composite armour is either impossible or very expensive.

## Originality

In the classic-car world, the term 'originality' is considerably overused and pretty much devoid of any real meaning. The moment a vehicle starts to be used it begins wearing out, and once the first factory component has been replaced the vehicle can no longer really be said to be 'original'. It might, just, be possible to find a civilian Land Rover that has been sitting in the back of a barn for the last 40 years and which, though shabby, remains much as it left Solihull. However, any military Land Rover will inevitably have been through at least one military rebuild programme which will mean that it cannot be described as 'original'. But looking at things from a slightly different perspective, it may be considered legitimate to describe a vehicle as 'original' if all of the parts remain correct for the year, or the month and year, in which it was constructed, even if they are replacement parts, or if parts have been replaced on a strict like-for-like basis, regardless of the date of manufacture.

However, for most vehicles 'originality'

remains an impossibility, and a far more pragmatic approach to the restoration of a military Land Rover is to try to replicate how the vehicle might have been operated and maintained at a specified period during its service career. After all, no army has any interest whatsoever in maintaining a vehicle in what an enthusiast would regard as 'original' condition, but has every intention of keeping the thing running and able to fulfil the role for which it was designed. A Land Rover that has been restored to a 'genuine military' condition should include only genuine military parts where these are applicable. In other words, any part which was of military specification and which was unique to the vehicle as supplied should be replaced with an identical component – even though for the typical military Land Rover most of the parts are identical with their civilian equivalents.

You must make up your own mind about how far you want to go and whether or not you consider modern reproduction parts to be acceptable, but remember, no military vehicle should be fitted with civilian parts where military items were available originally.

## Restoration

Make no mistake – as with most vehicles, restoration can be a costly business. Military Land Rovers have generally yet to achieve the cult status of the Jeep, but

**RIGHT This signwritten 'FC 101' provided an excellent advertising vehicle for a business specialising in 4x4 vehicles.** *(Des Penny)*

nevertheless, at the time of writing a well-restored Series I can still cost £10–15,000. If your budget is more modest, vehicles can still be found at prices way below this, and parts availability is such that most Land Rovers can be restored. Engines, transmissions, wiring looms, instruments... everything remains available, and even the most badly rusted-out bulkhead or chassis can be repaired or replaced. However, remember that in the long run the cost of restoring a poor example will inevitably exceed the cost of buying a vehicle that has been well restored by someone else. It is good advice to buy the best example that you can afford, particularly in terms of the condition of the bodywork, and let the previous owner bear the cost of restoration.

Proper restoration will involve dismantling the vehicle right down to its individual parts and then replacing or repairing all worn, rusted and damaged components; and in the process it will be impossible to maintain any links that the vehicle has with its service past. If the vehicle remains sound and still has many of its original features you should therefore give serious consideration to maintaining it in that condition. This is what is described in some spheres as 'a state of arrested decay'.

**ABOVE** Not every ex-military vehicle ends up in the hands of a military-vehicle re-enactor, this colourful 'lightweight' being a good case in point. *(Phil Royal)*

**BELOW** Photographed in Algeria in 1995, this ex-RAF Series II ambulance, nicknamed 'Cheese Butty' for obvious reasons, is recovering a bogged-down Transit. The vehicle, which is owned by Rainbow Rovers, forms part of an aid convoy, and was left in Algeria at the end of the aid project for use by the refugees. *(Des Penny)*

**ABOVE Ex-RAF airfield fire-crash-rescue vehicle converted to a breakdown/recovery vehicle by Henderson's Garage, Alston, Cumbria.** *(Des Penny)*

**BELOW This would be the ultimate conversion for an ex-military Land Rover... if only it were ex-military!** *(Warehouse Collection)*

If you must restore but are still keen on maintaining a genuine 'military' appearance, be wary of over-restoring your own vehicle or of buying one that has been over-restored. Land Rovers have not always been chrome-plated and leather-trimmed with matching body cappings, and older vehicles were generally not perfect when they left the factory. Slight imperfections in the appearance of the body panels are perfectly acceptable, and some over-spray on the engine and components in the engine compartment is in order. Unnecessarily fussy detailing – for example picking out details in contrasting colours, or using self-adhesive vinyl lettering rather than stencilling – is an absolute 'no-no'.

When trying to decide how the vehicle should be finished and detailed, take a look at some genuine military vehicles in service. Note

particularly the multiple coats of often poorly applied thick green and black paint, and the lack of attention to detail!

The *Haynes Restoration Manual: Land Rover Series I, II and III* will be found particularly useful.

## Driving and handling

It would be fair to say that few current vehicles drive like a leaf-sprung Land Rover – it has its own peculiar combination of bone-jarring discomfort, combined with high levels of engine and wind noise. And as regards handling, whilst it might be fun it is also decidedly pedestrian. Indeed, the question of handling is almost academic – you don't buy a Land Rover for its road-holding, even if you choose one of the later models with coil springs. On all early models the ride is harsh and the steering vague, particularly to those more used to a modern rack-and-pinion set-up, with lots of turns of the huge wheel to get from lock to lock. The centre of gravity is high, which discourages over-exuberant cornering. For most variants acceleration is best described as 'acceptable', and although an older Land Rover will keep up with 'A road' traffic without too much difficulty, you won't be doing much overtaking.

Off the road it's a different matter altogether – a Land Rover will go practically anywhere it is pointed and is both surefooted and communicative, able to pick its way across obstacles like a mountain goat.

From the driver's seat the steering-wheel position is a tad old-fashioned, but the pedals are large and nicely placed, allowing operation by boot-clad feet. The brakes are good and the gearbox is positive, even if double-declutching is occasionally required for downshifts. If the front wheels are not properly balanced there may be a vibration at certain speeds. As to the comfort side... well, on the older models there is little conventional comfort at all. The seat cushions are thin and the backs lack any proper lumbar support, and this, combined with the cart-spring suspension and stiff-walled tyres, ensures that the occupants feel every bump in the road.

On early open-top vehicles the weather equipment is minimal, which makes it a fair-weather car. Providing the weather is warm and the traffic fairly light most people would no

doubt agree that an early Land Rover is fun to drive, but most military Land Rovers lack even a basic heater and in colder weather you will need to think very carefully about what you wear. If you plan to travel any distance you will almost certainly be thankful for thermal underwear, a hat with earflaps and good gloves.

And whilst insurance may be cheap if you are able to opt for a collector's policy, the beast's fuel consumption means that you will constantly be putting your hand in your pocket.

## Safety

Let's face it, neither the safety of the occupants nor that of luckless pedestrians that the vehicle might run into were high on the design team's list of priorities, and an early Land Rover would achieve no Euro NCAP stars for safety. As regards passive safety systems, forget it! There are plenty of sharp-edged projections on the dashboard and windscreen panel, and on most early models there are no seat belts or air bags and no crash padding at all. Proper seat belts can be fitted without too much difficulty, but the steering wheel remains too close to the driver's chest, although at least the steering box is tucked well behind the front axle.

The situation has changed considerably since 1948, and huge improvements have been made to the strength of the body and the safety of the interior. Nevertheless, NCAP figures for the late model Defender do not seem to be readily available. Even if they were they would not necessarily apply to the military versions, and it is only in the last few years that roll cages and safety harnesses have featured on British military vehicles.

On the road, handling can also be sufficiently wayward to catch out the unwary, and it is as well to remember that the wet-weather performance of the original 'bar-grip' style non-directional cross-country (NDCC) tyres is decidedly marginal, the lack of conventional tread meaning that surface water can build up under the tyre, causing aquaplaning. The performance can be improved without too much of a compromise in appearance by a process known as 'siping' whereby slits, or 'sipes', are cut into the tread bar perpendicular to the direction of rotation. The process, which is named after its inventor John

F. Sipe who patented the process in 1923, is popular with some off-roaders, and at least in the USA the process is offered by some tyre retailers, who use a so-called 'siping machine'. Hand siping tools can also be obtained, but using them is a laborious process. Check out 'www.sipers.com' for more information, but don't forget to tell your insurance company that your tyres have been modified.

## Tax and insurance

Any Land Rover that was built before 1 January 1973 will be classified as an 'historic vehicle' and will be exempt from vehicle excise duty in Britain. Similarly, any vehicle constructed before 1 January 1960 will also be exempt from the need for annual testing. In order to ensure that a previously unregistered military vehicle qualifies for the 'historic vehicle' tax class, and for test exemption, it will almost certainly be necessary to produce some documentary evidence of the date the vehicle was manufactured – the clubs or the British Motor Industry Heritage Trust (BMIHT, www.heritage-motor-centre.co.uk) should be able to help, providing you have the original chassis number or VIN (vehicle identification number).

A 'classic' Land Rover that is not used as everyday transport will also be eligible for classic-car insurance, but it is always a wise precaution to be able to prove the value of the vehicle, including those hard-to-find military accessories, before finally agreeing the insurance figure.

**BELOW Old Land Rovers never die!**
*(Des Penny)*

'This publication, primarily prepared for use in civilian workshops, has been approved for use in Army Workshops and is intended for the guidance of personnel responsible for the maintenance and overhaul of Rover Mk 1 and Mk 2 vehicles.'

**War Office code 18389, technical handbook** November 1958

## Chapter Ten

# The mechanic's view

Disregarding the late model Defenders that have complex electronics, the Land Rover is a relatively straightforward motor vehicle and is sufficiently old-fashioned to allow it to be maintained by the average home mechanic. At the same time it is also well built, reliable and perfectly capable of everyday use. The only real downside is that in order to keep the vehicle in peak condition much higher levels of regular maintenance are required than for the average modern car. However, all of the components are easily accessible and there is little need for specialised tools or equipment.

**OPPOSITE Some vehicles will always be beyond salvation.**
*(Ian Young)*

# Safety first

It hardly needs to be said that any motor vehicle can bite, and bite hard, if treated without sufficient respect. Even during maintenance and repair operations there are all kinds of potential perils, some of which can result in serious personal injury.

## Personal protection

- Before starting work, make sure you are wearing proper mechanic's overalls and stout boots or shoes, preferably with steel toecaps. Tuck any loose hair, neckties or other clothing out of harm's way. Remove rings or other jewellery to avoid the possibility of causing accidental electrical short circuits.
- Never work under a vehicle that is not properly supported on axle stands. A jack does not provide safe support.
- Keep your hands and fingers away from the fan when the engine is running. Be particularly wary of electric fans, which can start without any warning.
- Remember that the exhaust system and radiator become very hot when the engine is running and can cause skin burns.
- Do not attempt to lift heavy components without adequate assistance. A good rule of thumb is to not try to lift more than 120lb (55kg) single-handedly. The figure should be reduced if the load is awkward or sharp-edged, or if it needs to be held at arms' length, or if you are forced into an uncomfortable working position.
- Wear suitable eye protection when using a grinding wheel or powered abrasive discs, etc.
- Do not strip paints and surface coatings without proper respiratory protection. Old paints often contain lead compounds, which are potentially injurious, and some of the modern military infrared reflective paints also contain injurious compounds.
- Do not spray paints or other fluids without proper respiratory protection.
- Do not spray inflammable fluids in the presence of a naked flame.

## Potential hazards

- Never run the engine in a closed space. Carbon monoxide exhaust gases are poisonous and can cause permanent brain damage and death. Even a modern vehicle with a catalytic converter is only said to produce *less noxious* gases.

**RIGHT AND FAR RIGHT Rust in areas of the steel bulkhead is a problem with most Land Rovers. The first photograph shows corrosion in the hinge area; in the second shot the bulkhead has been patched.**
*(Warehouse Collection)*

- Battery acid is corrosive to metal and will burn skin and clothing. Make sure it stays inside the battery!
- The gases produced by an open-vented battery during charging and discharging are highly inflammable and can easily ignite.
- Be careful of short-circuiting the batteries. There is sufficient voltage and current available from 24V FFR vehicles to cause the battery casing to split, to start a fire in the wiring, or to cause serious skin burns.
- Petrol vapour is highly flammable, with a flashpoint of –40°C (–40°F), which means that it can ignite in contact with a naked flame under any normal ambient conditions. Do not expose such vapours to naked flame and never introduce any flame, or any apparatus that can produce a spark, into an empty fuel tank.
- Diesel fuel, and the fumes produced when the fuel is burned, are believed to be carcinogenic.
- Do not allow any fuels, oils or greases to come into contact with the skin; old engine oil, particularly, contains carcinogenic compounds. Wear disposable gloves or use a good skin barrier cream.
- Be careful not to accidentally put the vehicle into gear with the engine running, or to start it with first gear engaged.
- Dispose of used fluids in a responsible manner. Most local authority waste disposal sites have disposal facilities for old oils.

## Alternators

- If the vehicle is fitted with an alternator, this should be disconnected before undertaking any form of electric welding or cutting (arc, MIG, TIG, plasma cutting, etc).
- Likewise be careful of damaging delicate electronic components by short-circuiting.

## Tools and fasteners

Get hold of the proper military user manual, the maintenance manual and the parts list relating to your selected model. These books will repay you time and again in reducing frustration and wasted effort. Reproductions are often available and are preferable for use in the workshop anyway, since they are liable

to become well thumbed and greasy. Keep the originals indoors out of harm's way! If the handbooks indicate that special tools are required, try to find these at the military surplus dealers.

As regards the standard tools required for day-to-day maintenance, get hold of a good selection of imperial or metric 'AF' ('across flats') spanners and sockets, to suit the age of

**LEFT** Whilst the aluminium-alloy body panels do not rust, the soft metal can be easily distorted and will crack through work-hardening. It is common to find that the rubber doorstops on Series I vehicles have been broken out of the surrounding metal. *(Warehouse Collection)*

**BELOW** Land Rovers are simple and reliable machines – a fact that allows the military to subject them to all sorts of indignities. This Series I was photographed during extreme cold weather trials and it is unlikely that any civilian vehicle will be expected to start under these conditions! *(Warehouse Collection)*

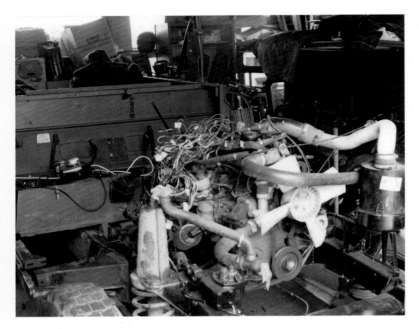

**ABOVE A complete strip-down will include removing the engine and transmission and, ultimately, the body.**

*(Ian Young)*

**BELOW Although beyond economic repair, a crash-damaged vehicle can still provide a useful source of parts.**

*(Ian Young)*

your vehicle. You will also need a lever-operated grease gun, and other standard hand tools such as pliers, feeler gauges, screwdrivers, hammer, etc. More specialised work will involve the use of a torque wrench.

On older Land Rovers the threaded fastenings use either American NF (SAE National 'fine') or NC (SAE National 'coarse') thread forms, more usually rendered as UNF and UNC. More modern vehicles will have metric threads and bolt sizes. It is always good practice to use new fasteners when reassembling parts after maintenance or

replacement, but pay particular attention that any replacements are made on a like-for-like basis as regards tensile strength.

# Maintenance and repairs

Unlike a modern car where bearings and bushes are sealed for life and service intervals have stretched beyond credibility, the older Land Rover requires regular attention from a grease gun to keep the suspension and steering bushes in peak operating condition. Similarly, the engine, transmission and other components need to be regularly checked and the oils changed or topped-up.

Find a copy of the appropriate lubrication chart and stick to the manufacturer's recommendations. Keep a proper record of the maintenance work.

# Day-to-day problems and reliability issues

Issues of comfort aside, a well-restored Land Rover, even an early example, should be sufficiently reliable for daily use. It certainly does not need nursing along, and there are few potential problems beyond those likely to be encountered with any older vehicle that has led a hard life and is only used infrequently. When choosing a vehicle to purchase, look for all the usual symptoms of a worn engine or transmission, including bottom-end knocking, excessive smoke, a slipping clutch or jumping out of gear, as well watching for the following general points:

### Engine
■ The use of anti-freeze is essential. If the water in the block has been allowed to freeze there will be almost certainly be damage to core plugs and the possibility of cracks in the block itself. Check carefully for staining or other evidence of cracks in the water jacket.
■ Over a period of time a damaged head gasket can result in serious corrosion to the cylinder head. Check that the compressions are all roughly equal.
■ Although the radiator is generously sized and should be able to cope with high

ambient temperatures, over a period of time it can become silted up, which will cause overheating problems.

■ Abusing the clutch in off-road situations can lead to breakage of the torque springs and possible damage to the faces of the driven plate and the flywheel.

## Transmission

■ A worn gearbox, or loose attachment of the bell housing to the engine, will cause the vehicle to jump out of second or third gear on the overrun. Some early vehicles may also exhibit a tendency to jump out of the low range on the transfer box.

■ Infrequent use of the four-wheel-drive system may lead to seizure of the operating mechanism.

■ If the vehicle has had freewheel hubs fitted, check that they can be properly engaged and disengaged and that the wheels rotate freely in the disengaged position.

■ Check the differential housings for signs of oil leaks.

■ Check the steering swivels for signs of corrosion in the housings, oil leaks, split gaiters (where fitted) and worn swivel pins.

**ABOVE This Wolf chassis might provide a sound basis on which to 'construct' a complete vehicle from a couple of wrecks.** *(Ian Young)*

**LEFT A large number of Snatch armoured vehicles have recently been released onto the surplus market. Some are lacking body panels, but as this photograph shows, replacement bodies – albeit well used – are available.** *(Ian Young)*

**ABOVE** The decision as to whether or not a vehicle is restorable will depend as much on its relative scarcity as its condition. This Series II/IIA ambulance is probably saveable, but it would be cheaper to find another that required less work. *(Ian Young)*

## Steering, suspension and brakes

■ Infrequent use of the vehicle will encourage seizure of the brake cylinders unless silicone brake fluid is used.

■ On leaf-sprung vehicles, check that the U bolts securing the axles to the springs are tight, and that there is not excessive play in any of the spring eye bushes.

■ If the steering seems excessively stiff or

heavy, check that the adjuster on the side of the steering box has not been over-tightened, and that the track rod ends and steering relay joints are well greased. Check that the power steering pump operates correctly on vehicles that are so equipped.

■ The handbrake is located behind the transfer case and is prone to oil contamination from failure of the rear seal. This will compromise

**RIGHT** Auctions often provide a useful source of used parts, but unfortunately you may have to buy more than you need and hope to sell the unwanted items at a later date. *(Ian Young)*

the operation of the brake and lead to MoT test failure.

## Wheels and tyres

- Check the wheels and tyres for signs of splits, cracking or other damage caused by age or careless off-roading.
- Some Series I and Series II/IIA vehicles were fitted with two-piece 'split rim' wheels which need to be dismantled to enable the tyres to be changed – your local 'Kwiktires' branch will not be best pleased, and unless you are a stickler for military authenticity you should consider replacing them with conventional well-base wheels.
- The early military 'bar-grip' style (NDCC) of cross-country tyre offers very little grip on wet roads. Again, you should consider whether the appearance of the vehicle has a higher priority than your personal safety.

## Electrical system

- The 24V electrical system of FFR vehicles has a bad reputation, but having twice the normal voltage available can be something of a bonus, minimising niggling earthing faults and ensuring reliable starting in sub-zero temperatures. However, the downside is that most electrical items will have to be purchased from military-surplus dealers, and a 24V 90Ah alternator will not be cheap!

## Bodywork

- Despite the widespread use of aluminium in the body, rust is still the big killer, particularly with early vehicles. The bulkheads tend to rust through, as do the top surfaces of the chassis, the outriggers, spring hanger attachment points, and cross-members.
- Check the aluminium outer panels for excessive surface damage and cracking.
- Series Is have no door stops beyond a simple rubber buffer on the side of the front mudguard. There will almost inevitably be splits and other damage to the mudguard where the door has been allowed to slam against it.
- Look carefully at areas where aluminium is in contact with steel, such as where the body is bolted to the chassis. Over time there will be sacrificial corrosion of the dissimilar metals.
- Puddles under the pedals or other evidence of a wet floor suggest that the door seals have hardened or that the doors or sliding windows (on early models) are not correctly fitted.
- A corroded doorframe will prevent the door from closing properly, as will worn striker plates.

# Epilogue

It is Land Rover's proud boast that 75 per cent of all of the vehicles constructed by the company survive to this day. Press advertising has attested that 'thousands still keep slogging away' and that 'no other vehicle of its kind offers the same value for money'. Even in military service the Land Rover exhibits extraordinary longevity, with the British Army Wolf Defenders, purchased back in 1996, expected to remain in service until 2030 – an extraordinary 35-year life.

And it's certainly worth repeating... this is not at all bad for a vehicle that was intended as an interim measure!

*(Phil Royal)*

# Appendix 1

## Identification

The original Land Rover was described by the British Army as 'Rover Mk 1' or, more often, simply as 'Rover 1'; and until 1971, when the Series III was introduced, subsequent modifications to what the Army saw as the vehicle's basic configuration were assigned incremental 'mark' numbers. Unfortunately there seems to have been little agreement on what constituted a significant change and this, more than anything, has been responsible for the confusing description of early military Land Rovers.

Having described the basic chassis configuration by means of the 'mark number', the individual vehicle type was designated by an individual FV (fighting vehicle) number. Thus the full description, or nomenclature, for the basic 'Mk 1' was 'truck, cargo, ¼ ton, CL (or GS), 4x4, Rover Mk 1; FV18001'. This was in line with standard military practice at the time and meant that the Land Rover was described in the same way as its better-specified equivalent, the Austin Champ, which was known as 'truck, ¼ ton, CT, 4x4, Austin, Mk 1; FV1801'.

### Table 1: Military 'mark' numbers

| Designation | Description |
|---|---|
| Rover 1 | Original Series I cargo vehicle with 80in wheelbase and 1,595cc F-head engine. The Series IIA 'lightweight' was also described as 'Rover 1'. |
| Rover 2 | Late-production 80in Series I, with 1,997cc F-head engine. |
| Rover 3 | 86in Series I, with 52bhp 1,997cc F-head engine. |
| Rover 4 | 107in or 109in Series I cargo vehicle, heavy utility (station wagon), mountain rescue, or special ambulance. |
| Rover 5 | 88in Series I, including the 4x2 'utility'. |
| Rover 6 | 88in Series II cargo vehicle. |
| Rover 7 | 109in Series II cargo vehicle, heavy utility (station wagon), or special ambulance. |
| Rover 8 | 88in Series IIA; suffix '/1' (eg, 'Rover 8/1') indicates that the rear differential and halfshafts are strengthened; suffix '/2' indicates that they are standard. |
| Rover 9 | 109in Series IIA cargo vehicle, heavy utility or special ambulance; again, suffixed '/1' or '/2' to indicate the presence of strengthened or standard axles. |
| Rover 10 | 88in upgraded Series IIA. |
| Rover 11 | 109in upgraded Series IIA. |
| Rover Series 3* | Military designation for Series III; military 'mark' numbers were subsequently abandoned. |

* There were few short-wheelbase standard Series IIIs in British Army service, since this role was catered for by the 'lightweight', and this seemed to result in both standard long- and short-wheelbase machines being referred to as 'Rover Series 3'.

# Table 2: FV numbers and nomenclature

| Series I | |
|---|---|
| FV18001 | Truck, ¼ ton, cargo, GS, 4x4; Rover 1, 2 and 3. |
| FV18002 | Truck, ¼ ton, cargo, GS, armoured, 4x4; Rover 3. |
| FV18003 | Van, 10cwt, airfield lighting maintenance, 4x4; Rover 3. |
| FV18004 | Car, heavy utility, LWB, 4x4; Rover 4. |
| FV18005 | Truck, ¼ ton, ambulance, special, 4x4; Rover 4. |
| FV18006 | Truck, ¼ ton, SAS, 4x4; Rover 3 and 5. |
| FV18007 | Truck, ¼ ton, cargo, GS, 4x4; Rover 4 and 5. |
| FV18007 | Car, ¼ ton, utility, GS, 4x2; Rover 5. |
| FV18008 | Truck, ¼ ton, ambulance, 2 stretcher, 4x4; Rover 4. |
| FV18009 | Truck, ¼ ton, MOBAT towing, 4x4; Rover 5. |
| FV18010 | Truck, ¼ ton, guards para, 4x4; Rover 3 and 5. |

| Series II, Series IIA | |
|---|---|
| FV18021 | Truck, ¼ ton, cargo, GS, 4x4; Rover 6. |
| FV18021 | Car, ¼ ton, utility, GS, 4x2; Rover 6. |
| FV18021 | Truck, ¼ ton, cargo, GS, mine protected, 4x4; Rover 6. |
| FV18021 | Truck, ¼ ton, WOMBAT, 4x4; Rover 6. |
| FV18022 | Truck, ¼ ton, airfield lighting maintenance, 4x4; Rover 6. |
| FV18023 | Truck, ¼ ton, helicopter starting, 4x4; Rover 6. |
| FV18024 | Truck, ¼ ton, cargo, GS, 4x4; Rover 8/1 and 8/2. |
| FV18025 | Truck, ¼ ton, cargo, FFR, 4x4; Rover 8/1 and 8/2. |
| FV18031 | Truck, ¼ ton, cargo, FFR-24V, 4x4; Rover 10. |
| FV18032 | Truck, ¼ ton, cargo, FFR-12V, 4x4; Rover 10. |
| FV18032 | Truck, ¼ ton, line-layer, 4x4; Rover 10. |
| FV18033 | Truck, ¼ ton, cargo, GS, 4x4; Rover 10. |
| FV18041 | Truck, ¾ ton, cargo, GS, 4x4; Rover 7. |
| FV18041 | Truck, ¾ ton, cargo, GS, mine protected, 4x4; Rover 7. |
| FV18042 | Car, utility, heavy, 4x4; Rover 7 and 9. |
| FV18043 | Truck, ¾ ton, ambulance, 2-stretcher, mountain rescue, 4x4; Rover 7. |
| FV18044 | Truck, ¾ ton, ambulance, 2-stretcher, 4x4; Rover 7. |
| FV18045 | Truck, ¾ ton, WOMBAT, 4x4; Rover 7. |
| FV18046 | Truck, ¾ ton, sensitivity test, SAGW number 2, 4x4; Rover 7. |
| FV18047 | Truck, ¾ ton, fire-fighting, airfield crash rescue, 4x4; Rover 9 and 11. |
| FV18048 | Truck, ¾ ton, computer, 4x4; Rover 7. |
| FV18049 | Truck, ¾ ton, computer, Blue Water, SSGW number 1, 4x4; Rover 7. |
| FV18050 | Truck, ¾ ton, fuse test equipment, Blue Water, SSGW number 1, 4x4; Rover 7. |
| FV18051 | Truck, ¾ ton, mine detector, 4x4; Rover 7. |
| FV18052 | Truck, ¾ ton, cargo, GS, 4x4; Rover 9/1 and 9/2. |
| FV18053 | Truck, ¾ ton, cargo, FFR, 4x4; Rover 9/1 and 9/2. |
| FV18054 | Truck, ¾ ton, ambulance, 2/4-stretcher, 4x4; Rover 7. |
| FV18055 | Truck, ¾ ton, ambulance, 2/4-stretcher, mountain rescue, 4x4; Rover 7. |
| FV18061 | Truck, ¾ ton, cargo, GS, 4x4; Rover 9 and 11 (see also Series 3). |
| FV18061 | Truck, ¾ ton, cargo, with winch, GS, 4x4; Rover 9 and 11 (see also Series 3). |
| FV18061 | Truck, ¾ ton, cargo, fitted for FACE, 4x4; Rover 9 and 11 (see also Series 3). |
| FV18062 | Truck, ¾ ton, cargo, FFR-24V, 4x4; Rover 9 and 11 (see also Series 3). |

| Series II, Series IIA (continued) | |
|---|---|
| FV18062 | Truck, ¾ ton, cargo, FFR-24V, mine protected, 4x4; Rover 9 and 11 (see also Series 3). |
| FV18063 | Truck, ¾ ton, gun radar calibration, 4x4; Rover 9 and 11 (see also Series 3). |
| FV18064 | Truck, ¾ ton, SAS, 4x4; Rover 9 and 11. |
| FV18065 | Truck, ¾ ton, ambulance, 2-stretcher, 4x4; Rover 9, 11 (see also Series 3). |
| FV18066 | Truck, ¾ ton, ambulance, 2-stretcher, mountain rescue, 4x4; Rover 9, 11 (see also Series 3). |
| FV18067 | Truck, ¾ ton, ambulance, 2/4-stretcher Mk 2, 4x4; Rover 9 and 11 (see also Series 3). |
| FV18068 | Truck, ¾ ton, ambulance, 2/4-stretcher Mk 2, mountain rescue, 4x4; Rover 9 and 11 (see also Series 3). |
| FV18069 | Truck, ¾ ton, fire fighting, airfield crash rescue, tactical, for driven axle trailer, 4x4; Rover 9 and 11. |

| Series III (military designation 'Series 3') | |
|---|---|
| FV18061 | Truck, ¾ ton, cargo, 4x4; Rover Series 3. |
| FV18062 | Truck, ¾ ton, cargo, FFR-24V, 4x4; Rover Series 3. |
| FV18063 | Truck, ¾ ton, gun radar calibration, 4x4; Rover Series 3. |
| FV18065 | Truck, ¾ ton, ambulance, 2-stretcher, 4x4; Rover Series 3. |
| FV18066 | Truck, ¾ ton, ambulance, 2-stretcher, mountain rescue, 4x4; Rover Series 3. |
| FV18067 | Truck, ¾ ton, ambulance, 2/4-stretcher Mk 2, 4x4; Rover Series 3. |
| FV18068 | Truck, ¾ ton, ambulance, 2/4-stretcher Mk 2, mountain rescue, 4x4; Rover Series 3. |
| FV18070 | Truck, ¾ ton, radar set, truck mounted, 4x4; Rover Series 3. |
| FV18071 | Truck, ¾ ton, cargo, 4x4; Rover Series 3. |
| FV18071 | Truck, ¾ ton, cargo, with winch, 4x4; Rover Series 3. |
| FV18072 | Truck, ¾ ton, cargo, FFR-24V, 4x4; Rover Series 3. |
| FV18073 | Truck, ¾ ton, ambulance, 2/4-stretcher Mk 2, 4x4; Rover Series 3. |
| FV18074 | Truck, ¾ ton, ambulance, 2/4-stretcher, mountain rescue, Mk 2, 4x4; Rover Series 3. |
| FV18081 | Truck, ¾ ton, cargo, 4x4, diesel; Rover Series 3. |

| Series IIA, Series 3 'lightweight' | |
|---|---|
| FV18101 | Truck, ½ ton, GS, 4x4; Rover 1. |
| FV18101 | Truck, ½ ton, GS, WOMBAT, 4x4; Rover 1. |
| FV18102 | Truck, ½ ton, GS, FFR-24V, 4x4; Rover 1. |
| FV18103 | Truck, ½ ton, utility, 4x4; Rover Series 3. |
| FV18104 | Truck, ½ ton, utility, FFR-24V, 4x4; Rover Series 3. |

| Forward-control '101' | |
|---|---|
| FV19009 | Truck, 1 tonne, 4x4, ambulance, 4-stretcher, LHD; Land Rover. |
| FV19010 | Truck, 1 tonne, 4x4, ambulance, 4-stretcher, RHD; Land Rover. |

| Others | |
|---|---|
| FV18501 | Truck, air-portable, general purpose (APGP), scheme A; Rover 9. |
| FV18601 | Truck, air-portable, general purpose (APGP), scheme B; Rover 9. |

## Table 3: Other designations and descriptions associated with military Land Rovers

| | |
|---|---|
| Beeswing | FC '101' mounting six Swingfire anti-tank missiles. |
| CAV | CAMAC CAV composite armoured Defender 110 patrol vehicle; fitted with V8 petrol engine (see also Snatch). |
| Centaur | Tracked vehicle based on Stage One and Defender 110; built by Laird (Anglesey). |
| Challenger | Prototype for new range of military utility vehicles based on Discovery platform. |
| DPV | Desert patrol vehicle based on Defender 110. |
| Dragoon | Armoured patrol vehicle based on Defender 110; built by Hotspur Armoured Products. |
| Hebe | High-capacity pickup based on Pulse ambulance. |
| Hornet | Armoured patrol vehicle based on Defender 110; built by Glover Webb. |
| Hussar | 6x6 armoured patrol vehicle based on Defender 110; built by Penman Engineering. |
| Huzar | 6x6 armoured patrol vehicle based on Defender 110; built by Marek Pasierbski, Poland. |
| Llama | Prototype for tactical utility heavy (TUH) role. |
| MRCV | Multi-role combat vehicle based on Defender 110; subsequently renamed RDV. |
| Perentie 1-ton MC2 | 1-ton 4x4 vehicle based on Defender 110; developed by Jaguar Rover Australia (JRA) for the Australian Defence Force (ADF). |
| Perentie 2-ton MC2 | 2-ton 6x6 vehicle based on Defender 110; developed by JRA for the ADF. |
| Pink Panther | Special Forces vehicle based on Series IIA (FV18064). |
| Pulse | Wolf XD-130-based ambulance. |
| RDV | Rapid deployment vehicle based on Defender 90, 110 and 130. |
| Remus | Midlife upgraded Wolf XD. |
| Sandringham Six | 6x6 conversion based on Series III Stage One; built by Sandringham Motor Company. |
| Sandringham S6, S6E | Armoured personnel carrier (APC) based on Sandringham 6; built by Hotspur Armoured Products. |
| Shenzi Mk 1, 2 | Armoured patrol vehicle based on Defender 110; developed for the Royal Ulster Constabulary (RUC); renamed Simba. |
| Shorland | Armoured patrol car series; built by Short Brothers. |
| Simba | Armoured patrol vehicle based on Defender 110; developed for the RUC. |
| Skirmisher | 4x4 armoured patrol vehicle based on Defender 110; built by Penman Engineering. |
| Snatch 1, 1.5 | CAMAC CAV composite armoured Defender 110 patrol vehicle; fitted with V8 petrol engine. |
| Snatch 2, 2A, 2B | Upgraded version of Snatch 1; fitted with 300Tdi diesel engine. |
| Snatch Vixen | Upgraded version of Snatch 2A or 2B with heavy-duty axles and additional armour. |
| SOV | Special operations vehicle based on Defender 110; developed for US Rangers. |
| TACR-1 | Truck air crash rescue based on Series III. |
| TAC-T | Truck air crash with trailer based on Series III. |
| Tangi | Armoured patrol vehicle based on Defender 110; developed for the RUC. |
| Tenba Mk 1, 2 | Armoured patrol vehicle based on Defender 110; developed for the RUC; originally called Simba Mk 3. |
| Tithonus | Midlife upgraded Defender 110. |
| TUH | Tactical utility heavy; Land Rover offered the Llama for this role. |
| TUL | Tactical utility light; generic description of vehicles such as Defender 90. |
| TUM | Tactical utility medium; generic description of vehicles such as Defender 110, 127 and 130. |
| TUM (HD) | Tactical utility medium (heavy duty). |
| Vampire | FC '101' with electronic signals location equipment. |
| WMIK | Weapons mount installation kit (also refers to Land Rovers fitted with this kit); built by Ricardo Engineering. |
| Wolf XD | Heavy-duty military upgrade of Defender 90 and 110. |

**ABOVE Irish Defence Force Series IIA short-wheelbase utility vehicle. Note the extension to the windscreen header rail and the road-pattern tyres.** (*Sean O'Sullivan*)

**ABOVE** It is very unusual to find any documentary evidence of a vehicle's service career, but careful rubbing down of the paintwork may reveal markings that indicate the unit (or units) to which the vehicle was attached. This Series I carries both regimental and arm of service markings. *(Simon Thomson)*

## Table 4: Chassis numbering system

| Series I, Series II | |
|---|---|
| 1948–49 | Six- and seven-digit numbers, prefixed 'R' or 'L' to indicate right-hand or left-hand drive: first digit indicates year; second digit indicates Land Rover rather than car; third digit indicates variant (basic utility, station wagon or welder); last four digits are serial number. |
| 1950–53 | Eight-digit numbers, prefixed 'R' or 'L' to indicate right-hand or left-hand drive (1950 only): first digit indicates year; second digit indicates Land Rover rather than car; third digit indicates variant (basic utility, station wagon, welder or CKD kit for overseas assembly); fourth digit indicates home, LHD or RHD export market; last four (five for 1950 only) digits are serial number. |
| 1954–55 | Eight-digit numbers: first digit indicates year; second digit indicates Land Rover rather than car; third digit indicates variant (86in, 107in, 86in CKD, 107in CKD); fourth digit indicates home, LHD or RHD export market; last four digits are serial number. |
| 1955 | Nine-digit numbers: first digit indicates Land Rover rather than car; second digit indicates model; third digit indicates specification (home market, LHD export, LHD CKD, RHD export, or RHD CKD); fourth digit indicates sanction period; last five digits are serial number. |
| 1956–61 | Nine-digit numbers: first digit is 1; second and third digits indicate Series I (11–35) or Series II (41–70) and model; fourth digit indicates year; last five digits are serial number. |
| **Series IIA, Series III** | |
| 1962–79 | Eight-digit numbers with alpha suffix: first three numbers indicate Series IIA (241–354) or Series III (901–965) and model; last five digits are serial number. |
| **Series III, Defender, etc** | |
| 1980 on | 17-digit standardised international VIN (vehicle identification number): first three digits identify manufacturer; fourth and fifth digits indicate model; sixth digit indicates wheelbase length; seventh digit indicates body type; eighth digit indicates engine; ninth digit indicates steering position and transmission; tenth digit indicates model variant; eleventh digit indicates assembly plant (Solihull, or CKD); last six digits are serial number. |

# Appendix 2

## Technical specifications

### Series I

Typical nomenclature: truck, ¼ ton, cargo, GS, 4x4;
FV18001; Rover Mks 1–5.
Manufacturer: Rover Company Limited, Solihull,
Warwickshire.
Production: 1948–58.

Engine: Rover, four cylinders, 1,595cc, 50bhp, petrol. Rover,
four cylinders, 1,997cc, 52bhp, petrol. See Table 5.
Transmission: 4F1Rx2; part-time 4x4 (full-time 4x4 on early
models with freewheel).
Steering: recirculating ball, or worm and nut.
Suspension: live axles on multi-leaf semi-elliptical springs;
hydraulic double-acting telescopic shock absorbers.
Brakes: hydraulic; drums all round.
Construction: welded box-section steel ladder chassis; steel-
framed aluminium-panelled body.
Electrical system: 12V.

### Dimensions

Length: short wheelbase, 132–145in (3,353–3,683mm); long
wheelbase, 170in (4,318mm).
Width: 62in (1,575mm).
Height: open vehicles (top in place), 70–76in (1,778–1,930mm);
closed vehicles, 72in (1,810mm).
Wheelbase: 80in (2,032mm), 86in (2,184mm), 88in
(2,235mm); 107in (2,718mm), 109in (2,769mm).
Ground clearance: 8.5in (216mm).
Weight: short wheelbase, unladen 2,721lb (1,237kg),
laden 4,094lb (1,861kg); long wheelbase, unladen 3,240lb
(1,473kg), laden 4,899lb (2,227kg).

### Performance

Average maximum speed: road, 45mph (73kph); cross
country, 15mph (24kph).
Range of action: 220 miles (356km).
Approach/departure angles: 46°, 37°.
Fording depth: unprepared, 24in (610mm).

**Well-stowed Defender 110
photographed in the arena
at the War & Peace Show.**
(Phil Royal)

## Minerva TT

Typical nomenclature: truck, ¼ ton, cargo, 4x4; Minerva 'licence Rover' TT.
Manufacturer: Société Nouvelle Minerva SA, Brussels, Belgium.
Production: 1952–56.

Engine: Rover, four cylinders, 1,997cc, 52bhp, petrol. See Table 5.
Transmission: 4F1Rx2; part-time 4x4.
Steering: recirculating ball, or worm and nut.
Suspension: live axles on multi-leaf semi-elliptical springs; hydraulic double-acting telescopic shock absorbers.
Brakes: hydraulic; drums all round.
Construction: steel ladder chassis with pressed/fabricated-steel body.
Electrical system: 12V or 24V.

### Dimensions

Length: including jerrycan holder and rear-mounted spare wheel, 141in (3,581mm); without jerrycan and spare wheel, 129in (3,277mm).
Width: 61in (1,549mm).
Height: top in place, 74in (1,880mm); top and windscreen folded, 55in (1,397mm).
Wheelbase: 80in (2,032mm), 86in (2,184mm).
Ground clearance: 8.5in (216mm).
Weight: unladen 2,706lb (1,230kg), laden 4,004lb (1,820kg).

### Performance

Average speed: road, 55mph (89kph); cross country, 15mph (24kph).
Range of action: 195 miles (322km).
Approach/departure angles: 50°, 50°.
Fording depth: unprepared, 21in (533mm).

## Tempo/Land Rover Model 041

Typical nomenclature: field car, ¼ ton, 6 seater, 4x4; Tempo/Land-Rover.
Manufacturer: Vidal & Sohn Tempo-Werke GmbH, Hamburg-Harburg, West Germany.
Production: 1953–56.

Engine: Rover, four cylinders, 1,997cc, 52bhp, petrol. See Table 2.
Transmission: 4F1Rx2; part-time 4x4.
Steering: recirculating ball, or worm and nut.
Suspension: live axles on multi-leaf semi-elliptical springs; hydraulic double-acting telescopic shock absorbers.
Brakes: hydraulic; drums all round.
Construction: welded box-section steel ladder chassis with pressed/fabricated-steel body.
Electrical system: 12V.

### Dimensions

Length: including jerrycan holder and rear-mounted spare wheel, 147in (3,734mm); without jerrycan and spare wheel, 140in (3,556mm).
Width: 61in (1,549mm).
Height: top in place, 76in (1,930mm); top and windscreen folded, 56in (1,422mm).
Wheelbase: 80in (2,032mm), 86in (2,184mm).
Ground clearance: 8.5in (216mm).
Weight: unladen 3,135lb (1,425kg), laden 4,510lb (2,050kg).

### Performance

Maximum speed: road, 55mph (89kph); cross country, 15mph (24kph).
Range of action: 217 miles (352km), 435 miles (705km).
Approach/departure angles: 36°, 47°.
Fording depth: unprepared, 24in (610mm).

## Series II, Series IIA

Typical nomenclature: truck, ¼ ton, cargo, GS, 4x4; FV18021; Rover Mks 6–11.
Manufacturer: Rover Company Limited, Solihull, Warwickshire.
Production: 1958–71.

Engine: Rover, four cylinders, 2,286cc, 70bhp, petrol; four-cylinder. Other engine options not adopted by the British Army include Rover 2,052cc, 51bhp, diesel; and Rover four cylinders, 2,286cc, 62bhp, diesel. See Table 5.
Transmission: 4F1Rx2; part-time 4x4.
Steering: recirculating ball, worm and nut.
Suspension: live axles on multi-leaf semi-elliptical springs; hydraulic double-acting telescopic shock absorbers.
Brakes: hydraulic; drums all round.
Construction: welded box-section steel chassis; steel-framed aluminium-panelled body.
Electrical system: 12V or 24V.

### Dimensions

Length: short wheelbase, 142in (3,607mm); long wheelbase, 175in (4,445mm).
Width: 64in (1,626mm).
Height: open vehicles (top in place), 78in (1,981mm); closed vehicles, 81in (2,057mm).
Wheelbase: 88in (2,235mm); 109in (2,769mm).
Ground clearance: 8.5 or 9in (216mm, 229mm), according to tyre equipment.
Weight: short wheelbase, unladen 2,900lb (1,318kg), laden 4,453lb (2,024kg); long wheelbase, unladen 3,294lb (1,497kg), laden 5,905lb (2,684kg).

### Performance

Maximum speed: road, 65mph (105kph); cross country, 30mph (48kph).
Range of action: 280–360 miles (454–583km).
Approach/departure angles: 47°, 29°.
Fording depth: unprepared, 20in (508mm).

## Series IIA, Series III 'lightweight'

Typical nomenclature: truck, ½ ton, GS, FFR-24V, 4x4; FV18102; Rover 1.
Manufacturer: Rover Company Limited, Solihull, Warwickshire.
Production: 1965–84.

Engine: Rover, four cylinders, 2,286cc, 77bhp, petrol. Diesel option also available. See Table 5.
Transmission: 4F1Rx2; part-time 4x4.
Steering: recirculating ball, worm and nut; optional steering damper on the drag link.
Suspension: live axles on multi-leaf semi-elliptical springs; hydraulic double-acting telescopic shock absorbers.
Brakes: hydraulic; drums all round; vacuum servo-assistance on Series III models.
Construction: welded box-section steel chassis; steel-framed aluminium-panelled body with demountable panels.
Electrical system: 12V or 24V.

### Dimensions

Length: assembled, 147in (3,734mm); stripped, 143in (3,632mm).
Width: assembled, 64in (1,626mm); stripped, 60in (1,524mm).
Height: assembled, 77in (1,956mm); stripped, 58in (1,473mm).
Wheelbase: 88in (2,235mm).
Ground clearance: 8.25in (210mm).
Weight: assembled, unladen 3,210lb (1,459kg), laden 4,450lb (2,023kg); minimum stripped weight, 2,660lb (1,209kg).

### Performance

Maximum speed: road, 65mph (105kph); cross country, 25mph (48kph).
Range of action: 350 miles (567km).
Approach/departure angles: assembled, 49°, 36°; stripped, 58°, 38°.
Fording depth: 20in (508mm).

## Santana Model 88 *Militar* and 109 *Militar*

Typical nomenclature: truck, 500kg, cargo, 4x4; Land Rover/ Santana Model 88 *Militar*.

Manufacturer: Metalurgica de Santa Ana SA, Linares, Spain.
Production: 1969–90 for Model 88 *Militar*; 1973–90 for Model 109 *Militar*.

Engine: Rover/Santana, four cylinders, 2,286cc, 70bhp, petrol. Rover/Santana, four cylinders, 2,286cc, 62bhp, diesel. Rover/Santana, six cylinders, 3,429cc, 95bhp, petrol. Rover/Santana, six cylinders, 3,429cc, 92bhp, diesel. See Table 5.
Transmission: 4F1Rx2; part-time 4x4.
Steering: recirculating ball, worm and nut.
Suspension: live axles on multi-leaf semi-elliptical springs; hydraulic double-acting telescopic shock absorbers.
Brakes: hydraulic; drums all round.
Construction: steel ladder chassis with steel-framed aluminium body.
Electrical system: 24V.

### Dimensions

Length: short wheelbase, 146in (3,708kg); long wheelbase, 179in (4,547mm).
Width: 65in (1,651mm).
Height: open vehicles (top in place), 81in (2,057mm).
Wheelbase: 88in (2,235mm); 109in (2,769mm).
Ground clearance: 8.5in (216mm).
Weight: short wheelbase, unladen 2,974lb (1,352kg), laden 4,840lb (2,200kg); long wheelbase, unladen 3,615lb (1,643kg), laden 6,035lb (2,743kg).

### Performance

Maximum speed: road, 65mph (105kph); cross country, 30mph (48kph).
Range of action: 360–500 miles (583–810km).
Approach/departure angles: short wheelbase, 50°, 40°; long wheelbase, 52°, 31°.
Fording depth: with special equipment, 74in (1,880mm).

## Series III

Typical nomenclature: truck, ¾ ton, cargo, 4x4; FV18071; Rover Series 3.
Manufacturer: Rover Company Limited, Solihull, Warwickshire.
Production: 1971–85.

Engine: Rover, four cylinders, 2,286cc, 70bhp, petrol. Rover, four cylinders, 2,286cc, 62bhp, diesel. Other engine options not adopted by the British Army include Rover/Buick, V8, 3,528cc, 91–114bhp, petrol (Stage One only); and Rover, six cylinders, 2,625cc, 83–86bhp, petrol. See Table 5.
Transmission: 4F1Rx2; part-time 4x4.
Steering: recirculating ball, worm and nut.

Suspension: live axles on multi-leaf semi-elliptical springs; hydraulic double-acting telescopic shock absorbers; optional Aeon rubber helper springs.
Brakes: hydraulic; drums all round; optional vacuum servo-assistance.
Construction: welded box-section steel chassis; steel-framed aluminium-panelled body.
Electrical system: 12V or 24V.

### Dimensions

Length: short wheelbase, 142in (3,607mm); long wheelbase, 175in (4,445mm).
Width: 66in (1,676mm).
Height: 77in (1,956mm).
Wheelbase: 88in (2,235mm); 109in (2,769mm).
Ground clearance: 8.5in (216mm).
Weight: short wheelbase, unladen 2,953–3,097lb (1,342–1,408kg), laden 4,453–4,765lb (2,024–2,166kg); long wheelbase, unladen 3,301–3,455lb (1,500–1,570kg), laden 5,905–6,217lb (2,684–2,826kg).

### Performance

Maximum speed: road, 65mph (105kph); cross country, 30mph (48kph).
Range of action: 347 miles (560km).
Approach/departure angles: 46°, 30°.
Fording depth: 20in (508mm).

**ABOVE** The annual Defence Vehicle Dynamics Show, organised by the MoD Procurement Agency, continues to throw up interesting variations on the Land Rover theme... although this Snatch Defender, seen in 2009, attracts little attention from the trade and military personnel at the show. *(Warehouse Collection)*

## Defender 90, 110

Nomenclature: truck, utility, light (TUL), 4x4; truck, utility, medium (TUM), 4x4; Land Rover Defender 90, 110; originally described simply as Ninety and One-Ten.
Manufacturer: Land Rover Limited, Solihull, Warwickshire.
Production: 1983 on.

Engine: Land Rover, four cylinders, 2,286cc, 70bhp, petrol. Land Rover, four cylinders, 2,286cc, 62bhp, diesel. Land Rover/Buick, V8, 3,528cc, 114–134bhp, petrol. Land Rover, four cylinders, 2,495cc, 83bhp, petrol. Land Rover, four cylinders, 2,495cc, 85bhp, turbocharged diesel. Land Rover 200Tdi, four cylinders, 2,495cc, 107bhp, turbocharged diesel. Land Rover 300Tdi, four cylinders, 2,495cc, 111bhp, turbocharged diesel. Land Rover Td5, five cylinders, 2,493cc, 122bhp, turbocharged diesel. Other engine options not generally offered to military customers include Ford/Mazda Puma Duratorq Td4, four cylinders, 2,402cc, 122bhp, turbocharged diesel; and Ford, four cylinders, 2,198cc, 122bhp, turbocharged diesel. See Table 5.

**ABOVE Enthusiasm for military vehicles is not confined to Britain, and there are collectors in Australia, North America and right across Europe. This Series III ambulance was photographed at a military vehicle rally in Ireland.**
*(Warehouse Collection)*

Transmission: 5F1Rx2; full-time 4x4; centre lockable differential. 6F1R transmission also offered on commercial models.
Steering: recirculating ball, worm and nut; optional power assistance available.
Suspension: live axles on long-travel, dual-rate coil springs; axle location by Panhard rod at the front, and 'A' frame at the rear; hydraulic double-acting telescopic shock absorbers.
Brakes: dual servo-assisted hydraulic; discs all round.
Construction: reinforced welded box-section steel chassis; steel-framed aluminium-panelled body.
Electrical system: 12V or 24V.

### Dimensions
Length: short wheelbase, 153in (3,886mm); long wheelbase, 175in (4,450mm).
Width: 70in (1,778mm).

Height: 80in (2,032mm).
Wheelbase: 93in (2,362mm), 110in (2,794mm).
Ground clearance: 7.5in (190mm), 8.5in (216mm).
Typical weight: short wheelbase, unladen 3,729lb (1,695kg), laden 4,125lb (1,875kg); long wheelbase, unladen 4,717lb (2,144kg), laden 6,710lb (3,050kg). Actual weight varies according to engine and other equipment fitted.

### Performance
Maximum speed: road, 75–90mph (121–145kph); cross country, 35mph (57kph). Actual maximum speed varies according to engine fitted.
Range of action: 145–165 miles (235–267km).
Approach/departure angles: short wheelbase, 48°, 49°; long wheelbase, 50°, 35°.
Fording depth: 20in (508mm).

### Defender 127, 130
Nomenclature: truck, utility, medium, heavy-duty (TUM-H), 4x4; Land Rover Defender 127, 130.
Manufacturer: Land Rover Limited, Solihull, Warwickshire.
Production: 1984 on.

Engine: Land Rover, 300Tdi, four cylinders, 2,495cc, 111bhp, turbocharged diesel. Other engine options available for export only include Rover/Buick, V8, 3,528cc, 91–114bhp, petrol. See Table 5.
Transmission: 5F1Rx2; full-time 4x4; centre lockable differential.
Steering: recirculating ball, worm and nut; standard power-assistance.
Suspension: live axles on long-travel, dual-rate coil springs; axle location by Panhard rod at the front, and 'A' frame at the rear; hydraulic double-acting telescopic shock absorbers; co-axial helper springs at rear.
Brakes: dual servo-assisted hydraulic; discs all round.
Construction: reinforced welded box-section steel chassis; steel-framed aluminium-panelled body.
Electrical system: 12V or 24V.

### Dimensions
Length: 202in (5,131mm).
Width: 70in (1,778mm).
Height: unladen 80in (2,032mm).
Wheelbase: 127in (3,226mm).
Ground clearance: 8.5in (216mm).
Weight: unladen 4,589lb (2,086kg), laden 7,700lb (3,500kg).

### Performance
Maximum speed: road, 75mph (122kph); cross country, 30mph (48kph).
Range of action: 145 miles (235km).
Approach/departure angles: 50°, 35°.
Fording depth: 20in (508mm).

## Defender Wolf XD-90, XD-110
Nomenclature: truck, utility, light (TUL-HS), 4x4; truck, utility, medium (TUM-HS), 4x4; Land Rover Defender XD-90, XD-110 (Wolf).
Manufacturer: Land Rover Limited, Solihull, Warwickshire.
Production: 1996–2001.

Engine: Land Rover 300Tdi, four cylinders, 2,495cc, 111bhp, turbocharged diesel. Land Rover Td5, five cylinders, 2,493cc, 122bhp, turbocharged diesel. See Table 5.
Transmission: 5F1Rx2; full-time 4x4; centre lockable differential.
Steering: recirculating ball, worm and nut; optional power assistance available.
Suspension: reinforced live axles on long-travel coil springs; axle location by Panhard rod at the front, and 'A' frame at the rear; hydraulic double-acting telescopic shock absorbers.
Brakes: dual servo-assisted hydraulic; discs all round.

Construction: reinforced welded box-section steel chassis; steel-framed aluminium-panelled body.
Electrical system: 12V or 24V.

### Dimensions
Length: short wheelbase, 151in (3,835mm); long wheelbase, 179in (4,547mm).
Width: 70in (1,778mm).
Height: unladen 80in (2,032mm).
Wheelbase: 90in (2,286mm), 110in (2,790mm).
Ground clearance: short wheelbase, 9.5in (240mm); long wheelbase, 9in (230mm).
Weight: short wheelbase, unladen 4,400lb (2,000kg), laden 5,720lb (2,600kg); long wheelbase, unladen 4,717lb (2,144kg), laden 7,357lb (3,344kg).

### Performance
Maximum speed: road, 80mph (130kph); cross country, 35mph (57kph).
Range of action: 360 miles (583km).
Approach/departure angles: short wheelbase, 51°, 52°; short wheelbase, 51°, 35°.
Fording depth: 24in (610mm); with snorkel, 60in (1,525mm).

## Pulse XD-130
Nomenclature: truck, utility, medium (TUM-HS), field ambulance, 4x4; Land Rover Defender XD-130 Pulse.
Manufacturer: Land Rover Limited, Solihull, Warwickshire.
Production: 1996–98.

Engine: Land Rover 300Tdi, four cylinders, 2,495cc, 111bhp, turbocharged diesel. See Table 5.
Transmission: 5F1Rx2; full-time 4x4; centre lockable differential.
Steering: recirculating ball, worm and nut; optional power assistance available.
Suspension: reinforced live axles on long-travel coil springs; axle location by Panhard rod at the front, and 'A' frame at the rear; hydraulic double-acting telescopic shock absorbers.
Brakes: dual servo-assisted hydraulic; discs all round.
Construction: reinforced welded box-section steel chassis; steel-framed aluminium-panelled body.
Electrical system: 12V or 24V.

### Dimensions
Length: 204in (5,190mm).
Width: 70in (2,090m).
Height: unladen 101in (2,565mm).
Wheelbase: 127in (3,230mm).
Ground clearance: 9in (230mm).
Weight: unladen n/a, laden 8,230lb (3,741kg).

### Performance

Maximum speed: road, 80mph (130kph); cross country, 35mph (57kph).
Range of action: 360 miles (583km).
Approach/departure angles: 50°, 33°.
Fording depth: 24in (610mm); with snorkel, 60in (1,525mm).

## 1-tonne forward-control '101'

Nomenclature: truck, 1 tonne, 4x4, GS, forward control; FV19000 series; Land Rover.
Manufacturer: Rover Company Limited, Solihull, Warwickshire.
Production: 1972–74.

Engine: Rover/Buick, V8, 3,528cc, 128bhp, petrol. See Table 5.
Transmission: 4F1Rx2; full-time 4x4; positive lock on inter-axle differential.
Steering: recirculating ball, worm and nut; Woodhead steering damper.
Suspension: live axles on semi-elliptical tapered multi-leaf springs; anti-roll bar at front; double-acting telescopic hydraulic shock absorbers, uprated on the ambulance variant.
Brakes: servo-assisted dual-circuit hydraulic; drums all round.
Construction: welded box-section steel chassis with steel-framed aluminium-panelled body; body panels demountable to reduce overall weight.
Electrical system: 12V or 24V.

### Dimensions

Length: 162in (4,115mm).
Width: 72in (1,829mm).
Height: soft-top variants, 84in (2,134mm); hardtop variants, 94in (2,388mm).
Wheelbase: 101in (2,565mm).
Ground clearance: 10in (254mm).
Weight: unladen 4,233lb (1,924kg); laden 6,840lb (3,109kg); minimum stripped weight 3,500lb (1,591kg).

### Performance

Maximum speed: road, 62mph (100kph); cross country, 25mph (40kph).
Range of action: 350 miles (567km).
Approach/departure angles: 50°, 45°.
Fording depth: 24in (610mm).

## MC2 4x4 Perentie

Typical nomenclature: truck, 1,000kg, cargo, 4x4; Land Rover MC2.

Manufacturer: Leyland Australia Pty Limited, then Jaguar Rover Australia Pty Limited (JRA), North Ryde, NSW, Australia.
Production: 1987.

Engine: Isuzu 4BD1, four cylinders, 3,856cc, 84bhp, diesel. See Table 5.
Transmission: 4F1Rx2; full-time 4x4; centre lockable differential.
Steering: recirculating ball, worm and nut.
Suspension: reinforced live axles on long-travel, dual-rate coil springs; axle location by Panhard rod at the front, and 'A' frame at the rear; hydraulic double-acting telescopic shock absorbers.
Brakes: dual-circuit servo-assisted hydraulic; front discs brakes, drums at rear.
Construction: reinforced welded box-section galvanised-steel chassis; steel-framed aluminium-panelled body.
Electrical system: 12V.

### Dimensions

Length: 192in (4,877mm).
Width: 70in (1,778mm).
Height: to top of cab, 81in (2,057mm).
Wheelbase: 110in (2,794mm).
Ground clearance: 8in (203mm).
Weight: unladen 4,950lb (2,250kg); laden 7,040lb (3,200kg).

### Performance

Maximum speed: road, 72mph (117kph); cross country, 30mph (49kph).
Range of action: 280 miles (454km).
Approach/departure angles: 30°, 26°.
Fording depth: 24in (610mm).

## MC2 6x6 Perentie

Typical nomenclature: truck, 2,000kg, cargo, 6x6; Land Rover MC2 heavy-duty.
Manufacturer: Leyland Australia Pty Limited, then Jaguar Rover Australia Pty Limited (JRA), North Ryde, NSW, Australia.
Production: 1989–98.

Engine: Isuzu 4BD1-T, four cylinders, 3,856cc, 115bhp, turbocharged diesel. See Table 5.
Transmission: 4F1Rx2; full-time 4x4, selectable 6x6; centre lockable differential.
Steering: power-assisted variable-ratio worm and peg.
Suspension: reinforced live axles; long-travel, dual-rate coil springs at front, with axle location by Panhard rod; twin longitudinal dual-rate semi-elliptical multi-leaf springs linked

via shackles to cranked rocker beam at rear.
Brakes: dual-circuit servo-assisted hydraulic; front discs brakes, drums at rear.
Construction: reinforced welded box-section galvanised-steel chassis; steel-framed aluminium-panelled body.
Electrical system: 12V, 24V.

### Dimensions
Length: 242in (6,147mm).
Width: 81in (2,057mm).
Height: to top of cab, 82in (2,083mm).
Wheelbase: 120in (3,048mm); bogie centres, 35in (889mm).
Ground clearance: 7.75in (197mm).
Weight: unladen 8,052lb (3,660kg), laden 12,452lb (5,660kg).

### Performance
Maximum speed: road, 60mph (97kph); cross country, 25mph (41kph).
Range of action: 400 miles (648km).
Approach/departure angles: 37°, 25°.
Fording depth: 24in (610mm).

**BELOW** Although some 60 years separate the original Series I military Land Rover from this Defender 90 FFR vehicle, the family resemblance is unmistakeable. The Wilks brothers would be astonished to learn that their 'stopgap' vehicle has outlasted all of the company's other products. *(Simon Thomson)*

## Table 5: Basic engine data

| Description | Engine code | Date | Specification: cyls | capacity | bore x stroke | net power | max torque | Application |
|---|---|---|---|---|---|---|---|---|
| **Rover and Rover-derived engines** | | | | | | | | |
| 1.4-litre petrol | 10HP | 1947 | 4 | 1,389cc | 66.5 x 100mm | 44bhp at 4,400rpm | n/a | Early prototype |
| 1.6-litre petrol | Model 60 (12HP) | 1948 | 4 | 1,595cc | 69.5 x 105mm | 50bhp at 4,000rpm | 80lbf/ft at 2,000rpm | Series I |
| 2-litre petrol | 15HP | 1952 | 4 | 1,997cc | 77.8 x 105mm | 52bhp at 4,000rpm | 101lbf/ft at 1,500rpm | Series I, Minerva, Tempo |
| 2-litre diesel | 18HP | 1957 | 4 | 2,052cc | 85.79 x 88.9mm | 51bhp at 3,500rpm | 87lbf/ft at 2,000rpm | Series I, II |
| 2.25-litre petrol | 10H, 11H, 13H | 1958 | 4 | 2,286cc | 90.47 x 88.9mm | 70bhp at 4,000rpm | 124lbf/ft at 2,500rpm | Series II, IIA, IIB, III, lightweight, Defender, Santana |
| 3-litre petrol | 7L | 1959 | 6 | 2,995cc | 77.8 x 105mm | 110bhp at 4,500rpm | 153lbf/ft at 1,500rpm | 'Big lightweight', 101 FC prototype |
| 2.25-litre diesel | 10J | 1962 | 4 | 2,286cc | 90.47 x 88.9mm | 62bhp at 4,000rpm | 103lbf/ft at 1,800rpm | Series IIA, IIB, III, lightweight, Defender, Santana |
| 2.5-litre petrol | - | 1967 | 6 | 2,625cc | 77.8 x 92.1mm | 83–86bhp at 4,500rpm | 128–132lbf/ft at 1,500rpm | Series IIA, IIB, III |
| 3.5-litre petrol | - | 1973 | 6 | 3,429cc | 90.47 x 88.9mm | 95bhp at 4,000rpm | 177lbf/ft at 2,500rpm | Santana Model 109 *Militar*, S-2000 *Militar* |
| 3.5-litre diesel | - | 1973 | 6 | 3,429cc | 90.47 x 88.9mm | 92bhp at 4,000rpm | 153lbf/ft at 1,800rpm | Santana Model 109 *Militar*, S-2000 *Militar* |
| 3.5-litre petrol | - | 1979 | V8 | 3,528cc | 88.9 x 77.1mm | 91–114bhp at 3,500rpm | 166–185lbf/ft at 2,000rpm | Series III Stage One, Defender, 101 FC |

**RIGHT** 'Land Rover...
the best 4x4 by far.'
*(Phil Royal)*

| | | | | | | | | |
|---|---|---|---|---|---|---|---|---|
| 2.5-litre diesel | 12J, 13J, 14J, 15J | 1983 | 4 | 2,495cc | 90.47 x 97mm | 68bhp at 4,200rpm | 114lbf/ft at 1,800rpm | Defender |
| 2.5-litre petrol | 17H | 1985 | 4 | 2,495cc | 90.47 x 97mm | 83bhp at 4,200rpm | 133lbf/ft at 2,000rpm | Defender |
| 2.5-litre turbo diesel | 19J | 1985 | 4 | 2,495cc | 90.47 x 97mm | 85bhp at 4,350rpm | 150lbf/ft at 1,800rpm | Defender, Llama |
| 200Tdi turbo diesel | 11L | 1990 | 4 | 2,495cc | 90.47 x 97mm | 107bhp at 3,900rpm | 188lbf/ft at 1,800rpm | Defender |
| 300Tdi turbo diesel | 16L, 23L | 1994 | 4 | 2,495cc | 90.47 x 97mm | 111bhp at 4,250rpm | 195lbf/ft at 1,800rpm | Defender, Wolf Defender, Pulse, Otokar |
| Td5 turbo diesel | 15P, 16P | 1998 | 5 | 2,493cc | 84.45 x 88.95mm | 122bhp at 4,850rpm | 221lbf/ft at 1,800rpm | Defender |
| **Non-Rover engines** | | | | | | | | |
| Rolls-Royce | B40 Mk 2B | 1949 | 4 | 2,838cc | 88.9 x 114.3mm | 69bhp at 3,750rpm | 115lbf/ft at 2,150rpm | Series I B40 |
| Isuzu diesel | 4BD1 | 1987 | 4 | 3,856cc | 102 x 118mm | 84bhp at 3,200rpm | 180lbf/ft at 1,900rpm | JRA Series II, IIA, III, JRA Defender, Perentie MC2 4x4 |
| Isuzu turbo diesel | 4BD1-T | 1989 | 4 | 3,856cc | 102 x 118mm | 115bhp at 3,200rpm | 231lbf/ft at 1,900rpm | Perentie MC2 6x6 |
| Puma Td4 turbo diesel | - | 2007 | 4 | 2,402cc | 89.9 x 94.6mm | 122bhp at 3,500rpm | 268lbf/ft at 2,000rpm | Defender |
| Ford 2.2-litre turbo diesel | - | 2011 | 4 | 2,198cc | n/a | 122bhp at 3,850rpm | 268lbf/ft at 2,000rpm | Defender |

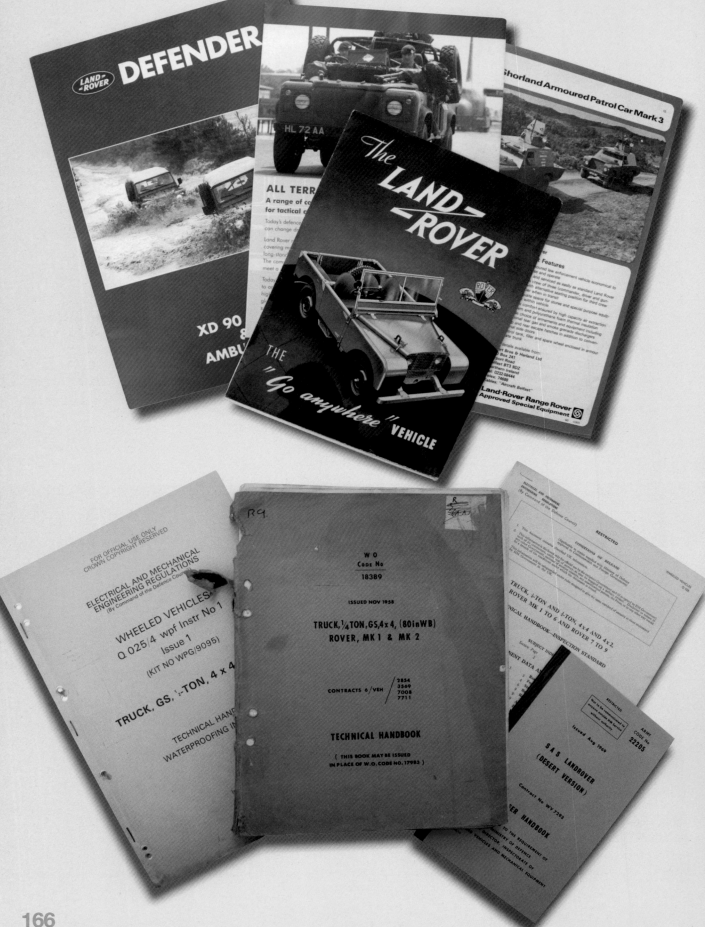

# Appendix 3

## Documentation

Like most British military vehicles, the Land Rover is the subject of an extraordinarily large volume of paperwork. Indeed, many enthusiasts actually seek out and collect official documents, manuals, photographs and other literature relating to their chosen vehicle. Aside from the sales brochures produced by Rover and Land Rover, the major official military publications fall broadly into the following groups, with literally dozens of individual documents produced. Tracking down copies of most of these is not as difficult as might be imagined:

- User handbooks.
- Technical descriptions.
- Miscellaneous instructions.
- Modification instructions.
- Waterproofing instructions.
- Inspection standards.
- Parts lists.
- Complete equipment schedules (listing all on-board equipment).
- Electrical and mechanical engineering regulations (EMER).
- Reports of field and user trials.
- Reports of user and troop trials.

It is almost certainly the same story with Land Rovers produced or used overseas.

### Other publications

There are literally dozens of books devoted to the Land Rover, which means that there is no shortage of additional reading material available. For the serious student, this small selection of titles will be found to provide useful information:

- *Combat Land Rovers: Portfolio No 1* by Bob Morrison. Brooklands Books, Cobham, 1999. ISBN 1-855-20604-8.
- *Haynes Enthusiast Guide: Land Rover Defender* by Martin and Simon Hodder. Haynes Publishing, Sparkford, 2010. ISBN 978-1-84425-710-2.
- *Haynes Restoration Manual: Land Rover Series I, II and III* by Lindsay Porter. Haynes Publishing, Sparkford, 1992. ISBN 978-1-85960-622-3.
- *Land Rover Military Portfolio* by Bob Morrison. Brooklands Books, Cobham, undated. ISBN 1-855-20561-0.
- *Land Rover: 60 Years of Adventure* by Nick Dimbleby. Haynes Publishing, Sparkford, 2008. ISBN 978-1-84425-498-9.
- *Modern Military Land Rovers in Colour 1971–1994* by James Taylor and Bob Morrison. Windrow & Greene Automotive, London, 1994. ISBN 1-85915-026-8.
- *Original Land Rover Series I: the Restorer's Guide to all Civil and Military Models 1948–58* by James Taylor. Bay View Books, Bideford, 1996. ISBN 1-870979-72-9.
- *Practical Classics on Land Rover Series I Restoration* Brooklands Books, Cobham, undated. ISBN 978-1-8552-0758-5.
- *The Half-Ton Military Land Rover* by Mark J. Cook. Veloce Publishing, Dorchester, 2001. ISBN 1-903706-00-9.
- *The Land Rover, 1948–1988: a Collector's Guide* by James Taylor. Motor Racing Publications, Croydon, 1984. ISBN 0-947981-25-X.
- *They Found Our Engineer: the Story of Arthur Goddard, the Land Rover's First Engineer* by Michael Bishop. Author House, Milton Keynes, 2011. ISBN 978-1-4567-7758-6.

**OPPOSITE TOP Over the years Land Rover has produced large numbers of military sales publications, which can be found at autojumbles and military-vehicle shows.** *(Warehouse Collection)*

**OPPOSITE BOTTOM As befits an essentially bureaucratic and procedure-driven organisation, the British Army produces prodigious amounts of paperwork, which many enthusiasts like to collect.** *(Warehouse Collection)*

# Appendix 4

## Useful contacts

### Internet

The best websites for military Land Rover enthusiasts are probably the 'Ex Military Land Rover Association' (www.emlra.org.uk), the 'Australian Register of Ex Military Land Rovers' (www.remlr.com), and 'Land Rover Madness' (www.lr-mad.co.uk). It is also worth checking out the 'Historic Military Vehicle Forum' (www.hmvf. co.uk), which, although broader based, frequently covers Land Rover-related topics.

### Purchases

All Ministry of Defence vehicle disposals are handled through Witham Specialist Vehicles, who, at least for the foreseeable future, should be considered the first port of call for buying newly-discharged surplus military Land Rovers.

Witham Specialist Vehicles
Limited
Honeypot Lane
Colsterworth
Grantham
Lincolnshire NG33 5LY
*Tel:* 01476 861361
*Website:* www.modsales.com

There are also plenty of military vehicle dealers around Britain, specialising in ex-military Land Rovers and parts.

Agricultural & Cross Country Vehicles
Belbroughton
Stourbridge
West Midlands DY9 0BL
*Tel* 01562 730404
*Website* www.defendercentre.com

Army Land Rovers
Dumfries
*Tel* 07920 763226
*Website* www.armylandrovers.com

Ashtree Land Rover International
5 Waterloo Terrace
Foundry Road
Anna Valley
Andover
Hampshire SP11 7LY
*Tel* 01264 333021
*Website* www.ashtreelandrover.com

Britpart – Border Holdings (UK) Limited
Craven Arms
Shropshire SY7 8DB
*Tel* 01588 672711
*Website* www.britpart.co.uk

Country Workshops
Risegate
Nr Spalding
Lincolnshire PE11 4EZ
*Tel* 01775 750223
*Website* www.british4x4centre.co.uk

DBR Military
Down Barn Farm
The Camp
Stroud
Gloucestershire GL6 7EY
*Tel* 07989 276713
*Website* www.milweb.net/dealers/trader/dbr.htm

Dunsfold DLR
Alfold Road
Alfold
Surrey GU8 4NP
*Tel* 01483 200567
*Website* www.dunsfold.com

John Richards
The Smithy, Hinstock
Market Drayton
Shropshire TF9 2TB
*Tel* 01952 550391
*Website* www.johnrichardssurplus.co.uk

L. Jackson & Company
Rocket Site
Misson
Doncaster
South Yorkshire DN10 6ET
*Tel* 01302 770485
*Website* www.ljacksonandco.com

LR Series
Unit 3, Brookfield Business Park
Shiptonthorpe
York YO43 3PU
*Tel* 01430 871590
*Website* www.lrseries.com

Marcus Glenn
Hope House, Hundreds Lane
Little Sutton
Nr Spalding
Lincolnshire PE12 9AJ
*Tel* 01406 364753
*Website* www.marcusglenn.com

P.A. Blanchard
Clay Lane, Shiptonthorpe
York YO4 3PU
*Tel* 01430 872765
*Website* www.pablanchard.co.uk

Shop4autoparts.net
Unit 1, 17 Lythalls Lane
Foleshill
Coventry CV6 6FN
*Tel* 024 7663 7337
*Website* www.shop4autoparts.net

# Glossary

**ACRT** – Airfield crash and rescue truck.
**ADF** – Australian Defence Force.
**APC** – Armoured personnel carrier.
**APGP** – Air-portable general purpose.
**APV** – Armoured personnel vehicle or armoured patrol vehicle.
**ATDU** – Amphibious Trials & Development Unit.
**ATGW** – Anti-tank guided weapon.
**ATMP** – All-terrain mobile platform.
**BAEE** – British Army Equipment Exhibition.
**CHF** – Commando Helicopter Force.
**CKD** – Completely knocked-down.
**DAS** – Demountable armour system.
**DERA** – Defence Evaluation & Research Agency.
**DPV** – Desert patrol vehicles.
**DROPS** – Demountable rack offload and pickup system.
**DVD** – Defence Vehicle Dynamics Show.
**EOD** – Explosive ordnance disposal.
**ERA** – Explosive reactive armour.
**FC** – Forward control.
**FFR** – Fitted for radio.
**FUT** – Fire unit truck.
**FV** – Fighting vehicle.
**FVDE** – Fighting Vehicle Development Establishment.
**FVRDE** – Fighting Vehicles Research & Development Establishment.
**GPMG** – General-purpose machine gun.
**GRP** – Glass-reinforced composite plastic.
**GS** – General service.
**GSR** – General Statement of Requirements.
**IDF** – Israeli Defence Force.
**IED** – Improvised explosive devices.
**IFF** – Identification friend or foe.
**IFOR** – Implementation Force.
**IFS** – Independent front suspension.
**IOE** – Inlet-over-exhaust.
**JATE** – Joint Air Transport Establishment.
**LHD** – left-hand drive.
**LML** – Lightweight multiple launcher.

**LRDG** – Long Range Desert Group.
**MDBF** – Mean distance between failure.
**MERT** – Medical emergency response team.
**MILAN** – *Missile d'infanterie léger anti-char*.
**MOBAT** – Mobile battalion anti-tank.
**MRCV** – Multi-role combat vehicle.
**MVEE** – Military Vehicles and Engineering Establishment.
**NDCC** – Non-directional cross-country tyres.
**OTAL** – One-ton amphibious Land Rover.
**RARDE** – Royal Armaments Research & Development Establishment.
**RAWS** – Rangers' anti-tank weapon system.
**RCLR** – Recoilless rifles.
**RDV** – Rapid deployment vehicle.
**REME** – Royal Electrical & Mechanical Engineers.
**RHD** – Right-hand drive.
**RN/BAEE** – Royal Navy and British Army Equipment Exhibition.
**ROPS** – Roll-over protection system.
**RSOV** – Rangers' SOV.
**RUC** – Royal Ulster Constabulary.
**Sipes** – Slits cut into tyre tread.
**SLR** – Self-loading rifle.
**SOV** – Special operations vehicle.
**SRDE** – Signals Research & Development Establishment.
**STANAG** – Standardisation agreement (NATO).
**TACP** – Tactical air command post.
**TACR** – Truck, aircraft, crash rescue.
**TAC-T** – Truck, aircraft crash, tactical.
**TES** – Theatre entry standard.
**TUH** – Truck, utility, heavy.
**TUL-HS** – Truck, utility, light, high specification.
**TUM-HS** – Truck, utility, medium, high specification.
**VIN** – Vehicle identification number.
**VPK** – Vehicle protection kit.
**WMIK** – Weapons mount installation kit.
**WOMBAT** – Weapon of magnesium, battalion anti-tank.

# Index

1-tonne forward-control  48
    ambulance  50
    technical specifications  162
'101', see 1-tonne forward-control

Air-portable general service (APGP)  42
Akrep  90, 119
Aluminium alloy, use of  13
Ambulances
    1-tonne forward-control  50, 61
    Defender  62
    field expedient  58
    Pinzgauer  64
    pod  63
    Pulse  63
    RAF crash-rescue  59
    Santana 109  61
    Series II  60
    Series IIA  60
    Series III  60
American Bantam, development of
    Jeep  10
Amphibians  42
    lightweight  106
    OTAL  98
    Portuguese 1-ton  100
Amsterdam Motor Show  13
Anti-tank weapon systems
    Carl Gustav recoilless rifle  66
    M40A1 106mm recoilless rifle  47, 65
    MILAN  50, 68
    MOBAT  66
    Nimrod  69
    Rangers anti-tank weapon system  66
    RAWS  66
    TOW  69
    US Rangers  66
    Vigilant  67
    WOMBAT  43, 66
APGP
    Scheme A  42
    Scheme B  44
Appliqué armour  70
Armor Holdings  73
Armour
    appliqué  70
    CAMAC CAV 100  70
    Defender 110 APC  88
    Dragoon  89
    Glover Webb APV  88
    Glover Webb Hornet  88

Hobson Industries Ranger  73
Hornet  88
Hotspur Dragoon  89
Hotspur Sandringham  89
Hussar  90
MACOSA BMU-2  89
Makrolon  70
Northern Ireland VPK  70
Otokar Akrep  90
Penman Engineering Hussar  90
Penman Engineering Skirmisher  90
'Piglet'  126
Shorland patrol car  90
Skirmisher  90
Snatch  70
Vehicle protection kit  70
VPK  70
WZP Huzar  92
Armoured personnel carriers
    Akrep  90, 119
    Defender 110 APC  88
    Dragoon  89
    Glover Webb APV  88
    Glover Webb Hornet  88
    Hornet  88
    Hotspur Dragoon  89
    Hotspur Sandringham  89
    Otokar Akrep  90, 119
    Sandringham  89
Austin
    Champ  29, 104, 124
    Gipsy  124

B40 engine, Rolls-Royce  102
Bache, David  17
Barton, Tom  12
Bashford, Gordon  12
Beeswing anti-tank missile  50, 68
'Big lightweight'  99
Bonallack & Sons  59
Boyle, Robert  12
British Army service  123
British Jeep  28
Broadhead, Mike  43
Buick V8 engine  21
Busby, Norman  43
Bushmaster, powered trailer  49, 99
Buying  132

CAMAC CAV 100 armour  70
Carawagon command vehicle  73

Carl Gustav recoilless rifle  66
Carmichael Redwing FT/6  76
Centaur half-track  92
Centre-steer prototype  12
Challenger  102
Champ  29, 104, 124
Champ, replacement  31
Chassis numbers  155
CKD kits  32
Command car
    Series I  98
    Carawagon  73
Communications role  36
Contacts  168
Conversion, military  57
County station wagon  22
Coventry Sewing Machine
    Company  8
Cullen, John  12
Cuthbertson four-track  93

DC100 concept vehicle  39
Defender
    90  22
    110  22
    110 APC  88
    127  24
    130  24
    ambulance  62
    gun tractor  51
    technical specifications  159
    Wolf  52
    XD  52
Demountable armour system  73
Desert patrol vehicle  81
Documentation  167
DPV  81
Dragoon  89
Driving  140

Engines  164
    1,389cc IOE petrol  13
    1,595cc IOE petrol  13
    1,997cc petrol  17
    2,052cc diesel  17
    2,286cc diesel  18
    2,286cc petrol  18
    2,494cc petrol  24
    2,495cc diesel  24
    2,625cc petrol  20
    2,995cc six-cylinder petrol  18

200Tdi 24
3,528cc V8 petrol 19
300Tdi 25
B40 102
Buick 19, 21
Ford Falcon 49
Isuzu 115
jet turbine 8
Meteor 8
Meteorite 8
Perkins Phaser 110T 95
Puma Td4 25
Rolls-Royce B40 102
Rolls-Royce Meteor 8
Td5 25
Turner diesel 103
ENTAC anti-tank missile 69
Esarco multi-wheeled vehicles 94
Experimental military vehicles 97

Fasteners 145
FFR 36
Fire-fighting role 73
    Carmichael Redwing FT/6 76
    fire-crash-rescue 74
    HCB-Angus Firefly 77
    TACR-1 74
    TAC-T 74
Firefly 77
Fitted for radio 36
Ford Motor Company 10
Forward-control
    '101' 48
    1 1/2-ton 99
    1-tonne 48
    Llama 101
    Series IIA 19
    Series IIB 19
FV numbers, list 153
FV1801 29

Glossary 169
Glover Webb
    APV 88
    Hornet 88
Glover-Esarco 94
Graham, F.W. 59
Gutty 28

Half-track, Centaur 92
Handling 140
HCB-Angus 74
    Firefly 77
Hebe, project 38
High-flotation wheels 105
Hobson Industries, Ranger 73
Hornet 88
HOT anti-tank missile 69

Hotspur 72
    Dragoon 89
    One Fifty 95
    Sandringham 89
Hover Rover 106
Hussar 90
Huzar 92

Identification 152
IFS 103
Independent front suspension 103
Insurance 141
Internet resources 168
Issigonis, Alec 28

Jeep 10
    British replacement 28
    CJ-2A 12
    in British Army service 124
    military surplus 12
JRA Perentie 115

Laird (Anglesey) 50, 92, 94
Licence-built military Land Rovers 109
    JRA Perentie 115
    Minerva 110
    Otokar 118
    Perentie 115
    Santana 113
    Tempo 111
Lightweight
    3/4-ton 99
    amphibian 106
    'big' 99
    Series IIA 45
    Series III 45
Line-layer role 77
Llama 101
Lusty, Ernie 72, 90

M40A1 106mm recoilless rifle 47, 65
Macclesfield Motor Bodies 63
MACOSA BMU-2 89
Maintenance 146
Marek Pasierbski 92
Marshalls of Cambridge 47, 60,
    61, 81
Masters, A.E. 30
Mercedes-Benz Gelandewagen 55
Meteor engine, Rolls-Royce 8
Mickleover Transport 60
Mid-life rebuild 38
MILAN anti-tank missile 50, 68
Military 'mark' numbers 152
Military trials 29
Minerva 32, 110
    technical specifications 157
Mini-Moke 45

Missiles
    Beeswing 50, 68
    ENTAC 69
    HOT 69
    MILAN 50, 68
    Nimrod 69
    Rapier 50, 51
    Swingfire 67
    TOW 69
    Vigilant 67
MOBAT anti-tank gun 66
Modification, military 31, 32
MoT test 141
MRCV 82
M-Type car, Rover 9
Mudlark 28
Multi-role combat vehicle 82
Multi-wheeled vehicles 94
MWG All-Terrain Vehicles 95

Nimrod anti-tank missile 69
Ninety, see Defender
Nuffield Mechanizations Gutty 28
Numbers
    chassis 155
    FV, list 153
    military 'mark', list 152

Operation Buffalo 127
One Ten, see Defender
Originality 138
Origins 10
OTAL amphibian 98
Otokar 118
    Akrep 90, 119
Overseas service 129

Pangolin 72
Park Royal Vehicles 60
Parts availability 136
Penman Engineering
    Hussar 90
    Skirmisher 90
Perentie 115
    technical specifications 162
'Piglet' 126
Pilcher-Greene 63
Pink Panther 79
Pinzgauer ambulance 64
Popp, Olaf 14
Portuguese 1-ton wader 100
Powered trailer 49, 99
Pre-production models 14
Price 134
Projects
    Hebe 38
    Llama 101
    Perentie 115

Remus 38
   Tithonus 38
Prototype, centre-steer 12
Pulse ambulance 63
   technical specifications 161
Purpose-built military vehicles 41
Pyrene 76

Ranger, Hobson Industries 73
Rangers
   anti-tank weapon system 66
   RAWS 66
   SOV 82
Rapid deployment vehicle 82
Rapier anti-aircraft missile 50, 51
RDV 82
Recoilless rifle
   Carl Gustav 66
   M40A1 106mm 47, 65
   Rangers anti-tank weapon system 66
   RAWS 66
Redwing 77
Reliability 146
Remus, project 38
Repairs 146
Replacement, DC100 concept
   vehicle 39
Reproduction parts 136
Restoration 138
Rolls-Royce B40 engine 102
Rover Cycle Company 8
Rover cars
   M-Type 9
   P3 9
   P4 9
Rubery Owen, powered trailer 49

Safety 141
   workshop 144
Sandringham Motor Company
   6x6 24
   APC 89
   Sandringham 6 95
   Sandringham Six 24
Santana 24, 113
   technical specifications 158
SAS
   Series I 78
   Pink Panther 79
Scottorn 76
   powered trailer 49, 99
Seager, Bob 46
Searle Carawagon command
   vehicle 73
Series I 15
   107in 16
   109in 16

80in 15
86in 16
88in 16
   ambulance 58
   command car 98
   SAS 78
   station wagon 16
   technical specifications 156
   Tickfords station wagon 15
Series II 17
   ambulance 60
   technical specifications 157
Series IIA 18
   ambulance 60
   lightweight 45
   lightweight, technical specifications 158
   Pink Panther 79
   forward-control 19
   technical specifications 157
Series IIB, forward-control 19
Series III 20
   ambulance 60
   lightweight 45
   lightweight, technical
      specifications 158
   Stage One 21
   Stage One Military V8 22
   technical specifications 158
Shanning Group 63
Shenzi 72
Shorland armoured patrol car 90
Short Brothers & Harland 92
Simba 72
Singapore Technologies Kinetics 63
Skirmisher 90
Snatch 70
SOV 82
Special Forces vehicles 78
   DPV 81
   Minerva 110
   MRCV 82
   Perentie 115
   Pink Panther 79
   Rangers' SOV 82
   RDV 82
   Series I 78
   SOV 82
Special operations vehicle 82
Specifications, see Technical
   specifications
Starley, John Kemp 8
Station wagons
   County 22
   military 4x2 31
   Series I 16
   Tickfords 15
Stonefield 124

Straussler, Nicholas 105
Swingfire anti-tank missile 67

TACR-1 74
TAC-T 74
Talbot-Darracq 32
Tangi 72
Tax 141
Technical specifications 156
   1-tonne forward-control 162
   Defender 159
   Minerva 157
   Perentie 162
   Pulse 161
   Santana 158
   Series I 156
   Series II 157
   Series IIA 157
   Series IIA lightweight 158
   Series III 158
   Series III lightweight 158
   Tempo 157
   Wolf Defender 161
Tempo 32, 111
   technical specifications 157
Tenba 72
Tickfords station wagon 15
Tithonus, project 38
Tools 145
TOW anti-tank missile 69
Tracked conversions
   Centaur 92
   Cuthbertson 93
Trials, military 29
Turner diesel engine, conversion 103

Vampire signals body 51
Vehicle protection kit 70
Vickers Hover Rover 106
Vidal & Sohn 112
Vigilant anti-tank missile 67
VPK 70

Wading, Wolf Defender 55
Walsh, G.P. 29
Weapons mount 83
   weapons mount installation kit 54, 84
   WMIK 54, 84
Wilks
   Maurice 8
   Spencer B. 8
Willys-Overland 10
WMIK 54, 84
Wolf Defender XD 52
   technical specifications 161
Wolseley Mudlark 28
WOMBAT anti-tank gun 43, 66
WZP Huzar 92